Photography: Randy Phillips and Hideaki Ogawa
Styling: Thomas Finch and Maira Berman
Thanks to: Tom Ligamari, Leighton Miller, Sumiko Phillips

Dedicated to Maira and Patti

Low Cost High Tech

Tibor Kalman
Danny Abelson
Eden Graber

A Wallaby Book Published by Simon & Schuster, New York

All prices are as of Fall 1980. Many of these
prices will rise in the course of time.

Published by Wallaby Books
A Simon & Schuster Division of Gulf & Western Corporation
Simon & Schuster Building   1230 Avenue of the Americas   New York, New York 10020
WALLABY and colophon are trademarks of Simon & Schuster
Designed by Carol Bokuniewicz and Amy Lipton for M&Co.
First Wallaby Books printing February 1981
Manufactured in the United States of America
1 3 5 7 9 10 8 6 4 2

Library of Congress Cataloging in Publication Data

Kalman, Tibor.
   Low cost high tech.

   1. House furnishings. 2. Interior decorating—
Amateurs' manuals. I. Abelson, Danny; Graber, Eden; joint authors.
II. Title.
TX311.K34   645   80-26225
ISBN 0-671-79148-6

CONTENTS

- Introduction —————— 9
- Living ———————— 14
- Sleeping ——————— 38
- Washing ——————— 54
- Food ————————— 68
- Working —————— 112
- Kids ———————— 124
- Access ——————— 140

We would like to thank the following for their invaluable help and advice: Jules Brandell at C&H Equipment, John Dunham of Equipto, Ina Rothenberg at Professional Kitchen, Fred Shamlian of Arthur Thomas, Jerry Schneider of Stan Deutsch and Abolite, Jim Leahy, Jr., of American Hotel Register, Micky and Ben Markovitz of DaRoma, J. Mike Kaiter of Import Specialists, Jean Deragon and Kim Agnew of Conran's, Steven Cayne of Cayne Equipment, Dory Winnick at Crown, Dan Richardson of Shure Mfg., as well as the helpful staffs at Thunder & Light, CE Glass and Times Square Lighting.

There was a time when it was considered bad manners to mention money in public, let alone on the cover of a book. But then that was when no-brand supermarket items and generic drugs seemed like a silly idea, and consumer education was thought to be only of interest to Olympic-class bargain hunters.

That's all changed, and not just because of a declining economy, though that may be the single largest factor. It has to do with quality as well. The idea that only good products make it to the marketplace is hardly taken seriously anymore. Too often these days when you've thrown away the handy new carry-home container, the product inside somehow doesn't work like it did in the commercial.

It goes on. Furniture for kids is no longer cheap in price but cheaper than ever in construction. The same applies to wooden bookcases and tables: the same money that used to buy a well-made and decently finished piece of furniture now pays for a poor-quality, unfinished object that looks like it was thrown together in ten minutes. In fact, if you take

a look at the entire range of furnishings for the home—from the department store TV stand to the etagere sold at the local housewares store—you realize that there has to be a better way.

There is, and as usual help comes from an unlikely source. The phrase High Tech was first used to describe the work of a group of architects who were using industrial components in nonindustrial settings, and using them in an unapologetic, undisguised way. To oversimplify, this idea was extended by interior designers to encompass a range of industrial products from airport landing strip lights to hospital faucets. They "discovered" a world of well-made products that had been there all along but now had a part to play in this new movement.

And that's where we come in. But while the department stores are now packaging the trendy High Tech *look*, we've headed in the opposite direction. This book is *not* about a look—it's about a rich source of inexpensive products that represent alternatives to the overpriced, overpackaged merchandise that most of us simply can't afford to buy anymore. We've focused on products sold to professionals—equipment used in hotels and classrooms, warehouses and hospitals, offices and art studios—that make sense for the home.

The $100 limit is not just a sales gimmick. We've gone so far as to cut many favorites because we expected their prices to rise over $100 by our publication date. In fact, when we did a final price check we asked suppliers about expected price increases and then quoted the higher figure in the book. But of course we can do nothing to stop prices from rising, and all we can say is that if there was a way to guarantee that all the prices quoted here would remain fixed for a year, we would have leaped at it.

This book should also help you save money in a quite different, less direct way. You'll notice that there is much talk of design and hardly a mention of decoration. We hope to further encourage the new interest in design, not in the arty, name-dropping sense but in the sense of a more realistic basis for making decisions about your home and the objects within it.

There's nothing that elevated or mysterious about interior design: how a room

works, how space can be used, what different forms of storage offer—these are the basic considerations it all comes down to. Thinking along these lines doesn't make sense merely from a design perspective, but is also, to put it dramatically, a matter of economic survival.

Speaking of survival, you will also be making decisions about safety. The responsibility for deciding whether the planned use of a product is appropriate or safe, particularly important when it involves electricity or children, rests with you. As authors we can suggest new possibilities, but we cannot guarantee the safe use of an item in your home.

The "I don't know much about it but I know what I like" attitude is all very well—until you have to buy expensive storage systems to make a crowded apartment feel larger, because you're mystified about how to best use your space. Or until your new furniture falls apart because you were more concerned with how it looked than with how it was made. In short, only the wealthy can afford to decorate—the rest of us need to think about design before we buy.

But that's not to imply that this is the last word on interior design or, for

that matter, on low-budget furniture or the High Tech movement. It's only a start, a sampling of what's out there. Which is not to say this is one of those expensive-looking interior design books that's virtually useless in practical terms. We cut out many items for every one that we included, and instead of flattering the objects by showing them in stunningly impressive, expensively designed surroundings, we shot every picture in a photographer's studio. An information caption accompanies every picture, and you can refer from this to the Access section, which is arranged by both type of products and by distributors (who we made sure *will* deal with you, *and* in small quantities).

We hope this book will serve as a map to territories which may be foreign to you. We also hope, to put it more pompously, that you'll look at things through slightly different eyes after reading it. But we knew it was first essential to make sure that it was a usable catalog. Like all designers, we wanted the object we were producing to function properly—to work on its own terms—before it did anything else.

Many of us remember growing up in a home where the living room was out of bounds, and if the custom of reserving a space for formal occasions has lapsed, it's not just because these are more casual times. Few of us live in homes so spacious that we can afford to rope off whole areas. But to go to the other extreme—to give up the idea of having a living room that is just a little more elegant and luxurious than the rest of the house—is also un-

Living

necessary. You can have it all, but only if you plan for it.

Those who have kids will find a room full of chrome and glass and white furniture as hard to neaten up for guests as those antique-filled stage sets of yesteryear. But you may be totally in love with that look and have no kids in your home: in the living room, as opposed to the kitchen or bathroom, individual needs are everything. There are no rules.

So, at the risk of being repetitive, the first thing you need to do is ask yourself some basic questions about the space. Does the whole family watch TV there? Do you often entertain large numbers of guests? How many feet of book shelves do you need, and how fast can you expect that figure to grow? You don't have to fill a notebook with data, but you do need to develop a reasonable sense of what you're working toward before you spend

your hard-earned dollars.

There are also no rules about taste, although few of us can truthfully claim that we're totally unaffected by fashion. These days, for example, arrangements which might have seemed cold or stark at one time look pleasingly unfussy and clean-lined—because we've *all* become accustomed to a less cluttered, simpler look.

But we're not trying to talk you into the High Tech aesthetic. As we said before, this book is

less about achieving a look than about affordable furniture that works right. Besides, most of these pieces taken individually won't impose a particular style on the decor all by themselves. They were designed, remember, for function rather than for fashion. The High Tech look will come and go, but flexible lighting, strong shelving and comfortable folding chairs are here to stay.

A note about couches: We had intended to bring couches within the price limit by describing ways in which they could be built. Despite our noble intentions, however, space limitations made only the most cursory outline possible, and we felt that that would be no better—and possibly even worse—than nothing at all. Store-bought couches these days cost only a little less than an art tour of Europe, and we certainly urge you to improvise and build your own. All you'll need is a little money, a little patience and, most important of all, a really thorough guide.

Solid Wood Pallet: Wood top, 18"w × 30"l, casters, $38.80. A. Liss. Coco Matting: One-sided herringbone pattern, 9' × 12', $76.00. Import Specialists. Crystallizing Dish: Laboratory glass, $21.34. Arthur A. Thomas.

For those accustomed to elaborate decor it's not always easy to see the elegance in simplicity. But this picture shows how handsome something as plain as a wooden pallet can look when used imaginatively. And if the lab glass (see page 87) and basket aren't to your taste, you could always view the pallet as a mobile platform for plants. The durable natural sisal flooring is a beautiful alternative to carpeting—which nowadays is too often both costly and poorly made.

This is one of our favorites—the pleasing and practical shallow dome yard light. Use a cord switch when mounting, then take a trip to the lighting section of your local department store and reflect smugly on how little they're offering for the price you've just paid.

Shallow Dome Yard Light: Porcelain enamel reflector in white (inside and out), aluminum hood, prewired, mounts on walls, 15" stem, bulbs up to 150 watts, $27.29. Appleton Electric.

Amaze your friends with your elegant lab glass vase, unusual lighting and thrillingly professional cart, then bore the pants off them with slides of your trip to Philadelphia. The cart, if we haven't said so before, is astoundingly strong—it rolls as easily when heavily loaded as it does empty.

Shallow Dome Yard Light: Porcelain-on-enamel reflector in white, aluminum hood, 15" stem, up to 150 watts, $27.29. Appleton Electric. **Pixmobile Mobile Machine Stand:** *Baked enamel in beige or aquamarine, ribbed black rubber top pad, 4" casters, 24"l × 18"w × 17"h, 12" from bottom to top shelf, $66.95. Electrical plug mold in red, $18.00 additional (add suffix "A"). Advance Products Company.*

All About Steel Shelving

Steel shelving, if you haven't already discovered it for yourself, is fabulously flexible and relatively inexpensive stuff. And contrary to the image you may have of drab gray metal, it's often available in a variety of bright colors and handsome finishes. In red for the kids' room, or black in the living room, it takes on an entirely different cast.

The first thing you need to know about it is that there are two basic grades. Industrial grade is 18 gauge or lower (the higher the gauge the *lighter* the metal) and is regulated by strict government standards. Commercial grade is 20 gauge or higher, and because the lighter commercial grade is unregulated it's also much more varied in quality. So

be wary of inexpensive shelving in department stores—it's often *dangerously* flimsy. We suggest you check that uprights are of 13 gauge or heavier metal, and you should also be sure you're getting angle rail uprights. The cheap imitations have uprights that look similar but are simply a flat strip of metal bent into a right angle, and they're much thinner. They do look the same, but that's where the similarity ends—thin metal strips just aren't strong enough.

Angle iron is not the only acceptable system. One alternative is "beaded post," which has a more tailored look: from a structural standpoint it's substantially the same, but it's much more expensive.

Almost all steel shelving operates on the same basic principles. The elements fit together with either clips or nuts and bolts. Some find nuts and bolts unwieldy, but we had no trouble with them and we do recommend

them for kids' rooms (see page 130). But have someone else there to hold the shelves as you fasten them.

Note the sway braces—thin diagonal bars—in the picture on page 113. These provide essential stability to the unit. The range of shelf sizes and positions is extremely wide, and you can buy accessories such as drawers or shelf dividers (called "bin dividers") for the units. Drawers cost about $6.00 each. Base covers, which give a unit a finished look, are about $1.50. In fact, there are other finishing touches which remove any vestige of steel shelving's industrial origins: post covers ($3.35) run the length of the uprights, covering the holes, and rubber tips (at a dollar apiece) fit over the feet.

Two last points: prices vary, even among distributors, so shop around. So also does the quality of the finish. Our recommendation is that when ordering colored shelving you state your preference for a factory finish—which will ensure that the distributor won't simply be repainting a gray unit. (We found Equipto and Able Steel to be reliable in terms of finishes—you may find others.)

A picture is worth a thousand words, particularly when it comes to overcoming a prejudice. Until you have new image to replace the old one of drab gray shelves, you just can't get all that enthusiastic about steel shelving. This basic unit has a black enamel finish, which, as you can see, makes all the difference in the world.

Steel Shelving Units: Angle post, 7'3"h × 36"w × 12"d, eight shelves, black enamel finish, $78.00. Drawers, $6.00; bin dividers, $2.00 @ additional. Able Steel Equipment. Clip-On Light "Reflex": Thermal plastic casing, reflector bulb, 30-, 50- up to 100-watt R-20, track or clamp-on, black, $31.50. Thunder and Light.

Skid Platform: Steel frame, wood top, 36"l × 30"w, $47.30. A. Liss. (Other sizes available.) **Radial Wave RLM's:** *Porcelain enamel, black or white, 20" diameter, about $55.00. Aboli.* **Nand Gopal Sisal:** *natural off-white, 4' × 6', $55.00. Import Specialists.* **Culture Flask** *(vase): 2 1/2 quart, $20.56. Arthur H. Thomas.*

The radial wave RLM hanging light is a descendant of a bygone street light, and widely held to be the aristocrat of industrial lights. It's not our idea of cheap, but by current standards it's a true beauty at a bargain-basement price. The steel-framed skid is also one of the handsomest creatures in its class. We still loved it after we lugged it home (it's heavy) and sanded the wood.

The 2 1/2-quart culture flask is much too curvy and graceful for its name, but then the people it's made for are not primarily interested in it for its good looks.

Wood Stacking Pallet: Steel angle frame, wood top, 24" × 24", $59.95. Mfg'd by Factory Service Co., available from C&H Distributors. **Enclosed Mercury Vapor Light:** *glass cover, aluminum, 175-watt reflector, about $80.00. Abolite.* **Coco matting:** *One-sided herringbone, 9' × 12', $76.00. Import Specialists.*

Even in its natural state, this stacking pallet has the kind of good looks that most sophisticated furniture stores strive for. But if you finish the wood you'll give it an even more dignified air, though you should sand it in either case. The clips on the rim of the hanging light's deep aluminum bowl hold its glass cover in place.

However patriotic you may be, you have to admit that the French do seem to attain a kind of effortless elegance in everything from food to clothes. These are very much like the chairs you find in French parks (hence the name). They're light, fold for storage, and—there's no avoiding it—are just a lot more stylish than the folding lawn chairs we're used to.

Folding French Park Chairs: Steel frame, wood back and seat, white, $61.00. Conran's.

*Windset Love Seat Glider: White steel frame, yellow vinyl lacing, 46" long, $74.48. American Hotel Register. **Windset Leisure Chair:** White steel frame, yellow vinyl lacing, $33.54. American Hotel Register. **Solid Wood Pallet:** 18" × 30", wheels, $38.80. A. Liss. (Other sizes available.)*

You're looking at the lawn furniture that hotels and resorts buy for themselves. The love seat swings and is surprisingly stable, but it's a bit harder to assemble than the chair.

*Versa-Tel Stacking Armchair: White aluminum frame, vinyl cross straps in yellow, blue or white, $67.14. American Hotel Register. **Wood Pallet:** Steel frame, wood top, 24" × 24", $59.95. Mfg'd by Factory Service Co., available from C&H Distributors. **Standard Dome RLM:** Porcelain on enamel, 14" diameter, white, green, yellow, blue, red or black, 150 watts, approximately $35.00. Abolite.*

The two stacking armchairs are no cheaper than most summer furniture, but these commercial models are definitely more solid. And that's important, because the only problem with using outdoor funiture indoors is that you often discover, once you get it inside, that it's just too flimsy. Please don't write to us about the orange—we flew a stylist in from Zurich to peel it that way, and as it cost us much more than the $100.00 limit we can't give you her name.

Paddock Bench: Black steel frame, green enamel finish or unpainted, 6' long, $99.99. Algoma Net Co. ***Plastic Radiator Filler:*** Red plastic, 3-gallon capacity, $11.70. Huffy Automotive.

With couches as pricey as they are nowadays, you might be willing to entertain other seating alternatives. Consider the trusty park bench, essentially unchanged these many years, and with good reason: there's little to improve on here. Solid oak and steel are strong and weather-proof, and the center leg makes this six-footer stable. Benches come green or unpainted, giving you the option of choosing your own color or better yet, staining it. And in case you overlooked the obvious, it's terrific outdoors.

Two folding chairs from the legendary L.L. Bean Catalog. The chair on the left was designed for low New England fireplaces and is, in fact, as stable as it looks. The catalog points out that you can fly-fish from it, which completely mystifies us.

The canoe chair on the right also folds flat. We don't know whether you can fly-fish from it, but it is beautiful and comfortable.

The square nylon basket can be used to hold magazines, firewood, or, in a pinch, fly-fishing equipment.

Fireside Chair: (left) Northern hardwood, 19" caned back and seat, 19" runners, $79.00. L.L. Bean. Canoe Chair: (right) Ash frame, caned back and seat, lightweight, $55.00. L.L. Bean. Square Basket: Steel frame, 2-bushel nylon basket in red, blue, green and other colors, $33.00. Steele Canvas Co.

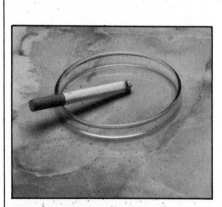

While we're reluctant to forge any association between science and smoking, allow us to offer this small suggestion. These little cuties cost around $20 for a dozen and make very handy and beautiful ashtrays. They are also so perfect as coasters that we suspect that their real function in the laboratory is as a resting place for scientists' cocktails.

Petri Dishes: Glass, 4" diameter, $20.20 per dozen. Arthur H. Thomas. (Other sizes available.)

Smith Victor Lamps: (left) 8" reflector, takes bulbs up to 250 watts. (center) 10" reflector, takes bulbs up to 250 watts. (right) 5" reflector, takes bulbs up to 100 watts. Light stand is black steel, extends 3–8', aluminum boom arm with counterweight is 44". Reflectors available in red, blue, yellow, green, brown and white, all $65.00. Available from Smith Victor dealers and Conran's.

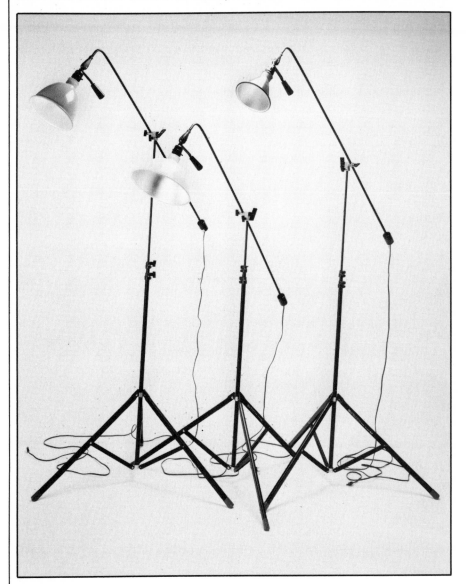

If there was ever a design category in which it made sense to pass up the decorators and stick with the professionals, it's lighting. You could wear out your shoe leather and your patience before you found anything like these beauties in a conventional lamp store.

Here we've shown three different shades, all of spun aluminum, mounted on a boom arm which is fitted with a counterweight, control handle and swivel socket. The base extends as much as 8 feet from a folded size of 3 feet. In terms of directional adjustment, this lamp is designed so you can turn it absolutely any way you want it. It's attractive, relatively inexpensive and light, and the icing on the cake is that the lamps come in a wide range of colors.

Theatrical Lighting

Having said at the outset that we're not interested in sexy looks and trendiness for their own sake, allow us to make an exception for theatrical lighting (nobody's perfect). No, it's not cheaper than other lighting, it's not really super-functional as residential lighting, and it's definitely not going to blend in with everybody's living room furniture. But, if you're ever going to fall for High Tech looks for their own sake, it'll probably be here.

The picture shows Fresnel spotlights on a light stand fitted with a T-bar. The spot on the right is fitted with "barn door" flaps, which give you control over the direction of the light. The Fresnel lights themselves adjust from a thin, strong "pin" beam to wider "flood" lighting.

In the picture we show one of the Fresnel spotlights mounted on a tripod. This is a lightweight yet sturdy structure which adjusts from 4 to 11 feet in height. The lights can also be mounted, by means of a U-clamp, flush against the wall or ceiling and on pipes as well as on tracks, or on a table base ordered separately. The light at center is a compact pin beam, which gives a narrow, clean shaft of light—excellent for highlighting—even though it's low voltage.

All the lights can be fitted with gels which create washes of light, but with or without gels this is dramatic—literally—and exciting light.

Fresnel Spot Lights: Black, 6" lens, medium socket, incandescent bulbs (250 watts), $57.00. Four-door barn door attachment, black, $27.75. Please see warning above concerning the cords for these lights. *T-Stand: Black weighted base, height adjusts 5–7', $38.00 T-Bar attachment, $15.00.* **Mounted Base** *(not shown): $11.25. All available at Times Square Stage Lighting.*

Two important notes: First-ly, make sure that the Fresnel lights you buy are modified to accept standard incandescent bulbs, and for some of the lights which have mogul sockets, you'll require a mogul to medium socket adapter (around $4.00 at hardware stores). Secondly, we were in error when we equipped the lights with coiled cords—they are *not* to be used with these lights.

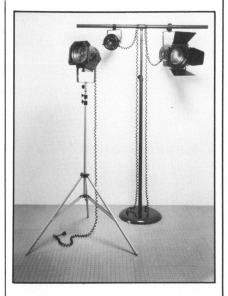

Fresnel Spot Lights: (left, on tripod; far right, on T-bar) Black, 6" lens, medium socket, incandescent bulbs (250 watts), $57.00. Four-door barn door attachment (far right), black, $27.75. Tripod: (left) Brushed chrome, height adjust 3–8', $61.50. Pin Beam Spot (hanging left on T-bar): Black, high-intensity, low wattage with transformer premounted in light, uses 25PAR 46 5.5-volt bulb, $50.50. Nonrolling Stand: Metal, 16" diameter base, height adjusts 4–11', $38.00. T-bar attachment, $15.00. All from Times Square Stage Lighting.

This shows a range of excellent clip-on lights—as opposed to bad clip-on lights, which are much easier to find.

From left to right: the first light is the Basik, which at $30.00 is one of the most expensive of the group. It has a rounded back and no exposed wires. Next is the Low Spot, which is more or less the same, but without the last two features. The larger Reflex has thermal plastic casing and looks like its design was influenced by theatrical lighting. Up top is a Low Spot fitted with a shade that enables you to use regular bulbs as opposed to the directional types used in the unshaded lights. The shades cost between $4.50 and $9.00. The two small wrinkle-necked lights are an impressive $13.50, and come in red and white, black and white, and all black. The last unit is also the first—it's the basic, fitted with a reflector shade.

You can get barn doors (see page 26) and color reflectors for many of these, and the shades on the Basik and Low Spot are interchangeable. Clip-ons don't have to look tacky, and unlike track lighting, require no installation and can be moved around at will.

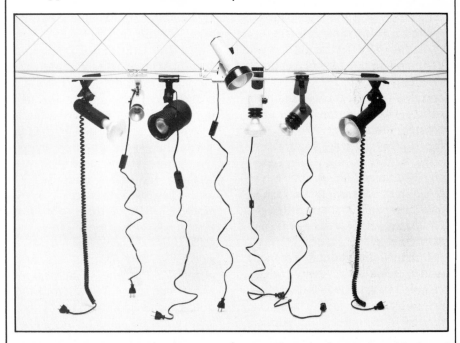

Clamp-On Lights—Basik: (extreme left and right): Plastic casing in black, beige or chrome, adjustable socket, available for track or clamp-on, uses up to 100-watt R-30 bulbs (about $3.50 each). Light, $29.95; reflector shade, $4.50. Low Spot: (second from left and center) Plastic casing in black, white, chrome and brass (additional), adjustable socket, $17.50. Uses up to 100-watt R-20 bulb (about $3.50). Reflector shade, $4.50. Available in other sizes; barn doors and larger reflector sizes additional. Reflex: (third from left) Thermal plastic casing, black, reflector bulb (up to 100-watt, R-20), track or clamp-on, $31.50. Gum Clamp-On: Plastic, red and white, black and white, all black (wire and clamp always black), takes up to 100-watt R-20 bulb, $13.50 plus bulb (about $3.50). All available from Thunder and Light.

A Brief Introduction to Three Construction Systems

If you're reasonably comfortable with simple construction, these are three alternative means of making table bases, closets, loft beds and shelving that you should know about. But if you're bewildered by a two-by-four, be aware that although these three systems have components which fit together easily, none of them is especially simple to design for. In either case you should find the following overview, incomplete though it is, of some interest.

The slotted angle shown here (and on page 29) is composed of components similar to the uprights of steel shelving, but with perforations that make for greater flexibility. We've used the smaller of the two available sizes, which, as you can see, isn't all that small. It comes to you unpainted, so you should turn to page 121 and look over the instructions on how to handle unpainted steel.

The Equipto Company (whose booklet on slotted angle, "Equiptogram 307," is the clearest guide we've seen) will send their slotted angle to you painted. It must generally be ordered in 100-foot lots at about $.95 per foot (plus 10% for painting), although you're likely to find a local dealer who will sell it in smaller lots. (Remember that a 3-foot cube will use 36 feet, so 100 feet is not all that much.) Slotted angle is incredibly strong and you can do practically anything with it—it's literally the grown-ups' erector set.

The Kee Klamp system is composed of pipes and clamps, though you buy the pipe at a plumbing supply store, as the company only makes the clamps. The name refers to the keylike Allen wrench which you use to tighten the bolts, called "set screws." 3/4-inch standard pipe at about $.60/ft. should be strong enough for most purposes, although clamps for pipes up to 2 inches in diameter are available.

The range of clamps is wide and includes angles, flanges and swivels enabling you to join pipes together in *many* different ways. They start around $2.00 each and average between $3.00 and $4.00. It's not incredibly cheap but its great virtue is the ease with which you can take it apart and rebuild with it: the loft bed you no longer need becomes a storage system you're desperate for. By the way, if you've heard of the Speed Rail system and it sounds similar, it is. So similar that we felt it was not necessary to describe Speed Rail separately.

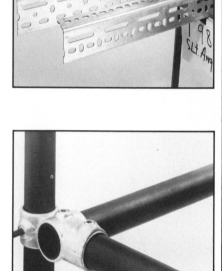

The third system is PVC piping, which consists of basic plastic plumbing pipe joined together by a special plastic solvent. You buy lengths (at $.62 per foot for the 1-inch pipe) which can be cut with a wood saw. Elbows and other joints cost between $1.00 and $2.00. It's usually white or gray, and comes in 1/2–2-inch diameters. The pipe you need will depend on the use, but you should err on the side of caution, i.e., order thicker pipe than is called for. This is extremely lightweight but strong stuff which costs little more than first-quality two-by-fours.

Somebody once noted that a little knowledge is a dangerous thing. What you've got here has the same relation to actual construction that an enthusiastic account of sky diving has to jumping out of a plane. Before you even *think* much more about this, get *all* the information you need.

This slotted angle frame has been fitted with steel shelves and is shown with a second slotted angle unit in its "home" beneath the shelves. The fact that you have to look twice before you realize the mobile TV stand is a separate object tells you something important: different components made of a common material go well together. You could try pressboard in place of plywood on the cart. The slotted angle, by the way, is factory finished in black.

Slotted Angle Home Entertainment Center: Slotted angle in black finish, with casters ($21.08 per set of four), two steel and two plywood shelves. Outer unit, 84"h × 48"w × 18"d (48 running feet); cart, 24"h × 47"h × 16"d (about 32 running feet), and two plywood shelves. Total unit price, $82.44. Equipto. Casters for cart, $21.08 additional.
"Basik" Clamp-On Lights: Plastic casing, black, beige or chrome, adjustable socket, available for clamp-on or track, uses up to 100-watt R-30 bulbs ($3.50), $29.95; reflector shade, $4.50. Thunder and Light.

Lakeside Cart: Stainless steel, 16 1/4"w × 27 3/4"l × 31 7/8"h, 3 1/2" swivel casters, 200-pound capacity, $80.50. Arthur H. Thomas. *Mondo Slate Tile Flooring:* Rubber, dark gray or burgundy, $3.90 per square foot. Allstate Rubber Corp.

You may not have heard of Lakeside but the hospitals, hotel and restaurant trades know them well. Because the rubber-bumpered cart is made of stainless steel, it's sleek enough to use in even the smartest living room. It's not a cheap material and in large amounts will tend to look cold and somehow institutional, but in balance with other elements, stainless steel is an extraordinarily good-looking metal, and it's certainly practical.

Reverse-Top Work-Storage Cabinet: Steel, baked enamel, gray, 24"l × 24"w × 34"h, two shelves, one adjustable, $87.77. *Mfg'd by Edsal, available from C&H Distributors. (Casters, $11.13 additional.)* **Standard Examining Lamp:** *Chrome, gooseneck head, height adjusts 54–73", $34.50. Arista Surgical Supply.* **Laboratory Glass:** *(vase) Hydrometer cylinder, 18" high, $22.61. (decanter) Erlenmeyer type flask, 2 1/2 quart, $12.24. Both from Arthur H. Thomas.*

These gray steel cabinets are not inexpensive, but they are indestructible. As liquor cabinets, they also serve to protect your supply against the three-year-old who has decided to sample your Napoleon Brandy to see what all the fuss is about. Needless to say, they can be used to house anything from china to stereo equipment.

Wall Storage Cabinet: Steel, gray baked enamel finish, 30"w × 12"d × 30"h, two shelves, steel pegboard doors, $49.97. Mfg'd by Homak, available from C&H Distributors. Cart: Steel, gray enamel finish, 30"l × 16"w × 32"h, 5" casters, $42.77. Extra shelf (shown), $9.34. Drawer (not shown), $9.96. Mfg'd by Edsal, available from C&H Distributors.

You're looking at two steel objects that we photographed "cold." We deliberately made little attempt to disguise or soften their appearance, because we feel that you should either accept them for what they are, or decide to give them a pass (though they can be painted, see page 121).

We happen to like their no-nonsense look. The cabinet's steel pegboard is every bit as useful as the masonite variety, but a lot better-looking. It also locks, has adjustable shelves, and in case anyone had any doubts, it's strong.

The cart, for all its boxiness, has a charm all its own, and just happens to be about half the price of the stainless steel Lakeside cart on page 30.

This maid's cart is equipped with decidedly unjanitorial supplies. The oversized back wheels make it stable and very easy to move, and of course you can adapt it to many other uses. Among other things, you could use it to move a buffet lunch from kitchen to back yard in one trip.

The tire tube test tank, used for testing punctured tires, also makes an excellent container for firewood.

Maid's Cart: Steel, silver blue hammertone finish, three shelves, 28"l × 23½"w × 41"h, $95.14. American Hotel Register. **Tire Tube Test Tank:** Steel, rolled edges, 31"l × 12"w × 12"h, $29.02. Huffy Automotive Products.

Van wheels have two obvious qualifications for the role of coffee-table base: they're the right height, and they have fabulous names. Can't you just hear the gasps of admiration as you point out the subtle difference between your Pantura Black Beauty and the Dynamo II?

We have two suggestions about how to get the most van wheel for your money. The first is that you look in junk yards and auto scrap yards for used wheels, and the second is that if you do buy them new you order the cheaper lightweight aluminum models. And while we're discussing options, you don't have to be as indulgent as we were with the table top—ordinary glass will do just as well as polished wire glass.

Van Wheels: (clockwise from left) The Magnus, 15" diameter, $67.00. Pantera Black Beauty, 15" diameter, $48.00. Dynamo II, 15" diameter, $53.00. Mfg'd by Superior, available from Max Finkelstein. (Not shown.) Plainer models available at Sears and J. C. Penney for about $20.00. **Glass Top:** Wire glass, baroque pattern, 20" diameter × ¹/₄" thick, $15.00. Mfg'd by C-E Glass, available at Capital Glass & Sash (or your local glass supplier, listed under "Glass" in the Yellow Pages). **Global Tile:** Rubber, ⁵/₃₂" thick, raised rubber disc surface, black, $2.98 per square foot; brown, terra cotta, green, gray or beige, $3.50 per square foot. U.S. Mat & Rubber.

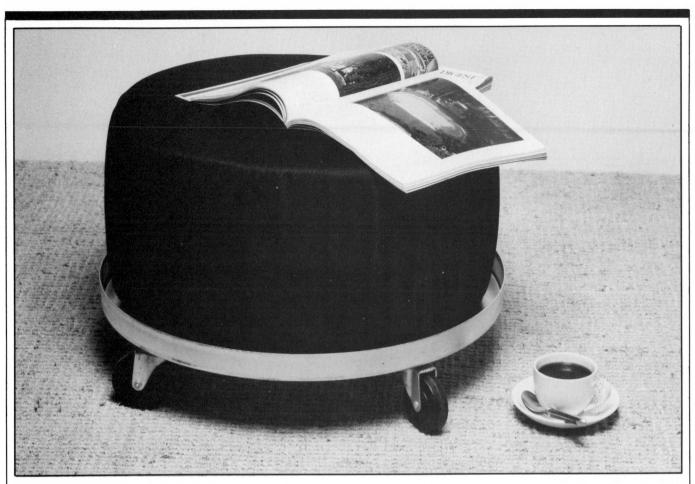

Foam: A high-density foam cylinder, 20½" diameter by 15" thick, approximately $18.00 from ABC foam. Covered with black upholstery fabric.

Steel Dolly: Steel platform zinc plated, 21" diameter, four 3" casters, $36.90. American Hotel Register.

We're showing this steel dolly fitted with foam to make a rolling ottoman, but you may well consider the dolly on its own merits. It makes a great plant stand, and you might want to use it as a low table in a platform seating area or any other close-to-the-floor arrangement.

Foam Couch: High-density foam seats; 24" × 24" × 16", $17.00 ea. Back piece, high-density foam, 72"w × 12"h × 4"d, $14.00. ABC Foam. Upholstery: movers' quilting, cotton blend, cotton batting filler, colors to match sample or basic, $9.00 per running yard (72" wide). Rennert.

This is the closest we could get to a real couch within our limit. There's an important qualification: if you make the same mistakes we did, you'll run over $100.00 Don't buy such thick squares, but instead use seats about 9 inches thick on a wooden or, better yet, identically upholstered platform. Order the thinnest movers' quilting available, and if you don't have a sewing machine handy, find somebody to make the covers up at a reasonable cost (we had our foam supplier make these for $25.00 apiece, but you may do better).

It's not a $1,000.00 couch for $100.00, but we felt it was worth going to the trouble of showing you what can be done with two inexpensive but durable materials.

The first person who thought of using movers quilts in the home ought to get some sort of award—it was a great idea. They've got the magic combination of qualities: strength, good looks and low price. They're covered in polished cotton, duck and cotton blends, and are warm enough to use as blanket and tough enough to cover furniture.

If you're going to use it for upholstery you should order it with thin cotton batting. Thicker quilts are fine for blankets but the stitching will tend to come out when used as upholstery.

The color range is almost infinite. Brown, black, green, beige, white, red, blue, navy and yellow, in light and dark shades, are the "standard" colors. However, if you send a color sample to Rennert, widely held to be the best of the bunch, they will do their best to match it. Quilts can also be ordered with different colors on each side, and though the standard pad is 6 inches by 76 inches, you can order yardage or pieces in virtually any length (76 inches is the maximum width) at $9.00 a yard.

To translate: pads in a stock color are $14.00 each, and in a specially matched and nonbasic color are $20.00 each. Rennert requests that you send a second choice of one of the basic colors each time you order custom colors. All pads are cotton blend, and are filled with cotton batting.

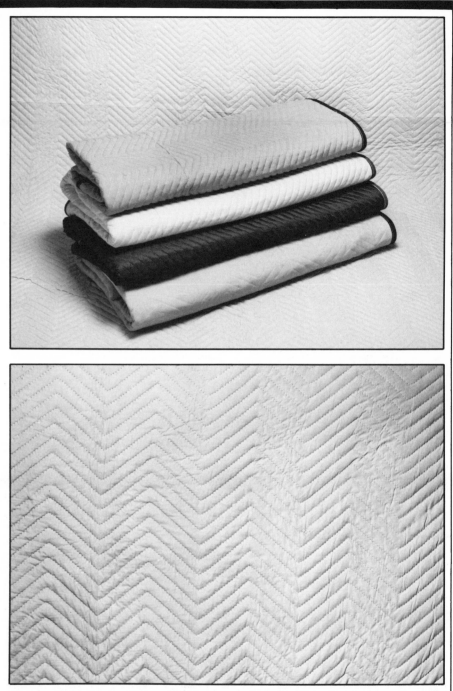

Movers Quilts/Pads: Cotton blends, cotton batting filler, herringbone (zigzag) pattern, edged in contrasting color, 76" × 68", $14.00 each in brown, black, green, beige, white, red, blue, navy and yellow; $20.00 each in custom colors. Yardage (76" wide), $9.00 per running yard. Rennert Mfg.

Sleeping

Chances are you've heard of someone with an incredible bedroom. It might feature 25 square feet of mirrored tile and a round satin-covered bed, or a 12-foot high multi-tiered tubular steel loft structure. Some people think that their bedrooms should be the uncensored expression of their wildest fantasies. And then there are the rest of us.

Don't think that we're opposed to individual taste or exotic decor if we address this chapter

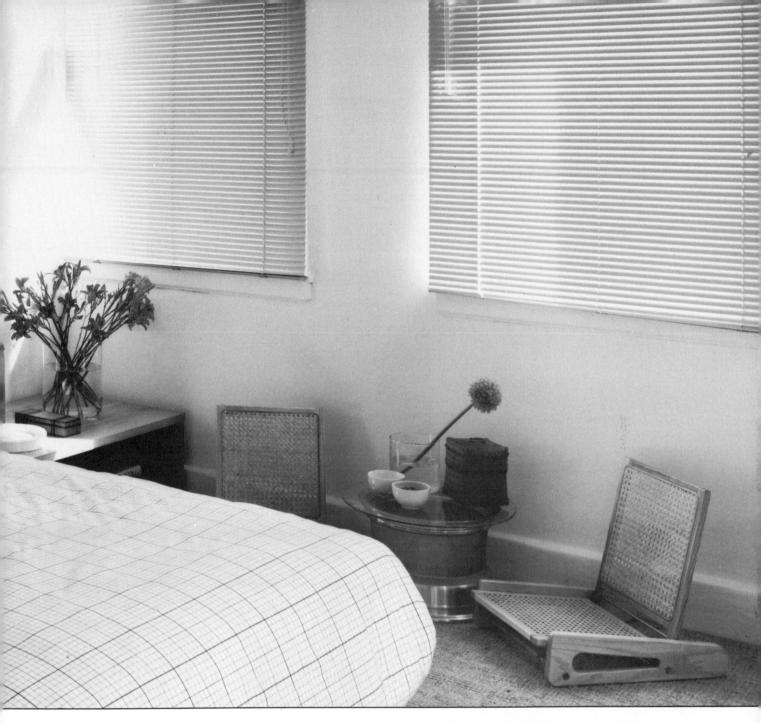

to people who have beds raised the conventional height off the floor, need a place to store their clothes, and lack a custom cabinet and lighting system built into the walls or headboards. It's just that there isn't space to cater to both groups in the same chapter (and who needs a book to be outrageous?).

So you'll have to contend with mundane considerations: lights that make sense for reading in bed, objects that adapt for bed-

side use, and inexpensive and compact bedroom storage systems.

Not surprisingly, some of the best bedroom furniture in the book is not in this chapter. If all goes according to plan, you will begin to see almost everything in here in terms of a whole range of possible uses, and the place in which a particular cart or chair appears will hardly matter at all. So if you're particularly interested in the bedroom, and

haven't done so already, we suggest that you look through the other chapters for items that could just as easily have been included here but weren't.

Mayo Instrument Stand: Chrome-plated steel, height adjusts 31–50", stainless steel tray (13" × 19"), casters, $65.50. Arista Surgical Supply.

There was a time when elegance meant velvet drapes and four-poster beds. Some people still refer to classical styles as embodying "timeless elegance" because, presumably, they outlasted their eras. But such elegance often ends up being anything but timeless—within years it's stuffy, overdone, dated: a victim of changing tastes.

This steel stand, because it is so utterly simple, is likely to be just as pleasing to your eye in ten years as it is today.

While these two folding chairs were originally intended for outdoor use they are certainly handsome enough for the home. Apart from their obvious advantages—they're light and easily stored—these low floor seats are surprisingly comfortable.

Fireside Chair: (left) Northern hardwood, caned back and seat, 19" runners, $79.00. L.L. Bean. Canoe Chair: (right) Ash frame, caned back and seat, lightweight, $55.00. L.L. Bean.

Remember when ads promised the product would make you "feel like a millionaire"? These hammocks may not make you feel any different, but they will give you a tenuous connection to the caviar-and-champagne-for-breakfast crowd. They're used as space-saving storage on boats, where even the super-rich need to think about such mundane matters.

Their obvious advantage is that they can be used practically anywhere, from a wall to a corner to a closet, to hold practically anything from towels to toys.

Gear Hammocks: 4' long, white or green, $6.25. Manhattan Marine.

The Museum of Modern Art in New York sells a beautiful overbed table designed by Eileen Gray. But you can also get this model from American Hotel Register. It incorporates the idea of the original, which is a great part of its beauty, and if this table is less refined than Gray's, it's also infinitely less expensive.

The examining lamp is adjustable, and a gooseneck is never a bad thing to have on a lamp, especially when you may want to direct the light away from the other side of the bed.

*Overbed Table: Walnut laminate top, stainless steel chrome-plated column and base, height adjusts 29–44", casters (not shown), $87.36. American Hotel Register. **Standard Examining Lamp:** Chrome, gooseneck head, height adjusts 54–73", $34.50. Arista Surgical Supply.*

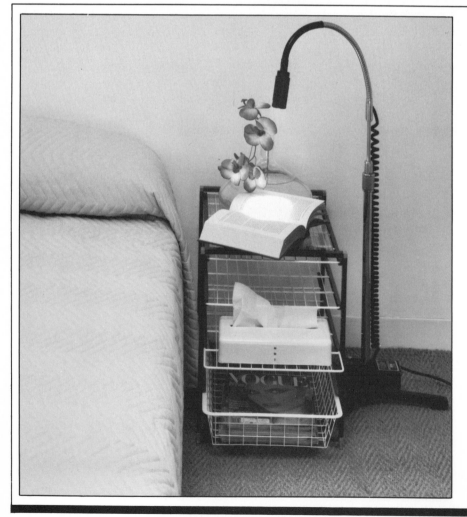

The Elfa frame in this picture proves our point—the chocolate brown metal and white wire is attractive enough to use anywhere. The light is a small indulgence, and we suggest you look at the price before you decide you *have* to own it. It's an examination light used by dentists and doctors, and thanks to a transformer built on to the base, projects a high-intensity light and is also energy efficient. A special lens enables you to adjust the beam from 1 inch to 5 inches in width.

The tissue dispenser also comes in chrome, and may be wall mounted.

*Night Table: Elfa, chocolate brown metal frame, 17 3/8" high, $30.00. Elfa, white, epoxy-coated wire baskets, $9.00 each. Scan Plast. **Tissue Dispenser:** White enamel, $5.54. American Hotel Register. (Chrome also available, slightly higher.) **Hi-Lo Examination Light:** High intensity, telescopic stand, flexible gooseneck head, low-cost longlife light bulbs, $99.00. Mfg'd by Goodlite, available from Central Dental Supply.*

Terrace Bench: Steel frame, wood seat and back, green or unpainted, 4' long, $81.00. Algoma Net Company. (Price includes UPS charges.) *Standard Examining Lamp:* Chrome, gooseneck head, adjusts 54–73", $34.50. Arista Surgical Supply.

Putting a bench at the foot of a bed is a sure sign that the mental boundaries separating "outdoor furniture" from "bedroom furniture" have dropped away. Once they have, it's difficult to remember that they were ever there, particularly when you see how handsome a $40 bench can look indoors.

The examining lamps are examples of a rare breed—simple, good-looking and functional lighting.

The same frame you've seen before but with different baskets. The one on top also fits in the frame for a one deep basket, one shallow basket arrangement. Four shallow baskets generally make more sense for drawer-type storage which we're combining with hanging space to make—in essence—a closet without walls.

Elfa Wire Baskets and Frame: Chocolate brown metal frame, 17 3/8 " h, $30.00. White epoxy-coated wire baskets, $9.00 each. All from Scan Plast.

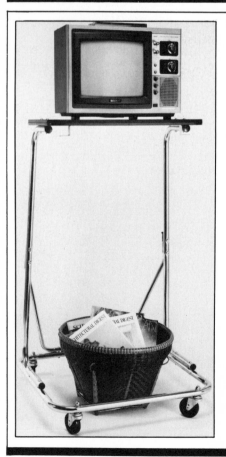

The various contraptions offered as TV stands and tables vary in shape and size but are similar in their almost uniform shabbiness. This one, which is designed for hospitals and rolls under the bed, is a stand worthy of the name.

Over-the-Foot TV Stand: Steel frame, wood shelf, 3" casters, 42" high, $57.95. American Hotel Register. (Holds up to 18" black-and-white and 17" color TV sets.)

Eldon Data Cart: Seven plastic shelves in black or beige, casters, aluminum reinforcements, $89.98. Crown Discount.

The fact that this cart serves as a bookcase and bedside table is not enormously surprising. That it looks so good is more impressive. The flexible-arm chart lamp projects a narrow beam, but we've decided not to recommend it because it has to be converted from 12 volts, and it's just not extraordinary enough to warrant the trouble.

Lockers: Metal, baked enamel finish in red, green, gray or tan, ventilation louvers. (left) Single-tier, with coat hooks and hat shelf, unit 12"w × 12"d × 60"h, approximately $68.00 per unit. (right) Double-tier, 12"w × 12"d × 60"h, approximately $79.00 per unit. Mfg'd by Penco, available from C&H Distributors. **Two-Drawer Tool Toter:** *Steel, baked enamel in gray, 2 1/2" casters, 14"w × 20"d × 32 1/2"h, $73.77. C&H Distributors.* **Extension Mirror:** *Normal/double magnification, 30" extension, $26.85. Brookstone.* **Surgical Dressing Jars:** *Between $4.00 and $5.00 depending on size. Arista Surgical Supply.*

You're looking at two sets of lockers, each three lockers wide. The single-tier lockers are on the left while those on the right are divided into two tiers. The advantages of each are obvious enough, and either way they provide the best closet this side of the mahogany six-footer that you inherited from a great-aunt. The two-drawer tool toter in front of the locker is here shown as a portable dresser which, if you're always late in the mornings, you might want to wheel to the bus stop with you as you finish dressing.

A complete dressing room can be put together from a few well-chosen items, none of them expensive, none requiring a room to house. The key is the collapsible wardrobe rack, useful here for the same reasons it makes an excellent winter-coat rack: it's high (over 5 feet) and wide (3½ feet) and it has storage racks above and below. Here we've used that space for clothes and shoes. In the hallway, the same racks serve for boots below and scarves, hats and gloves above. The clothes are stored in stackable transparent plastic containers, but that is only one of many options.

The companion piece is a wall rack with coat hooks, shelf and pole, which is built so that a series mounted together will look as tidy as one long unit. A series of these racks would comprise an instant closet all on their own.

A folding French park chair provides the kind of seating one wants in this type of area: it's solid, attractive and comfortable, but neither flimsy nor ridiculously cumbersome. A torpedo-shaped can with a 15-gallon capacity as a hamper makes it as easy to drop laundry into the right place (the hamper) as it is to drop it in the wrong place (the floor).

Collapsible Wardrobe Rack: Satin (matte) aluminum, top and bottom shelves, 6'1"h × 21"d × 3'6"l, $57.40. American Hotel Register. (Other lengths available.) Wall Rack with Coat Hooks: Satin aluminum, one 12" deep shelf, 3' long, $45.14. American Hotel Register. (Other sizes available.) Channel Frame Mirror with Shelf: Stainless steel frame, 16"w × 24"h, 5" deep shelf, approximately $22.00. Accessory Specialties. (Available in other sizes.) "Drop-In" Torpedo Waste Container: Steel, top opening, white, baked enamel, 15" diameter, $59.00. Mfg'd by Lawson, available from Beam Supply. Plastic Boxes: Clear plastic with lids, 15"l × 11"w × 6⅜"h, $5.75. Result. Folding French Park Chair: Steel frame, wood back and seat, white, $61.00. Conran's. Surgical Dressing Jars: Laboratory glass, between $4.00 and $5.50. Arista Surgical Supply.

*Steel Shelving: Floorking angle post, gray and colors (10% extra charge), 5'5"h × 36"w × 15"d, $39.00. Cayne Equipment. **Plastic Drawers:** (top shelves) Clear plastic with lid, 15"l × 10" × 3 1/2"h, $3.00. Stor-A-Drawer (third shelf), plastic sleeve box, beige and clear, $14.75. All from Result Mfg. **Elfa Wire Baskets:** (third shelf) Epoxy-coated white wire, $9.00. (bottom shelves) 21 1/4"l × 12 7/8"w × 11 1/4"d, $13.00. Scan Plast. (Other sizes available.) **Elfa Hall Racks:** (on wall, upper right) Epoxy-coated white wire, 11 3/4"w × 5 1/2"d, $13.00. Scan Plast (Other models available.)*

The plastic boxes at the top are used by department stores to display shirts and the like. Those on the middle shelf are slightly more sophisticated (and more expensive)—they slide, drawerlike, into beige plastic frames, which can be fitted together and joined by a plastic clip.

The flat Elfa basket is great for socks, handkerchiefs and the like, while the deeper baskets below offer more serious storage space.

The hall racks, hanging to the right, have to be, at $13.00 apiece, one of the real bargains of the Elfa line.

We claimed in our discussion of the preceding photo that this wall rack with coat hooks can be used on its own to make an instant closet. Here's living proof. It's only a simple, lightweight unit, but it has a shelf, hooks and a rod for hangers, and those are what make it so useful.

We've added two baskets from the Elfa system, and you should note that the deeper of the two is quite large enough to use as a laundry hamper. The hanging fluorescent light is a bit pricey but extremely useful—particularly as a portable, no-installation closet light.

Wall Rack with Coat Hooks: Aluminum rod and hooks, one 12" deep shelf, 3' long, $45.14. American Hotel Register. (Other sizes and two-shelf models also available.) Midget Light: Fluorescent, 8 watts, 14' coil, $32.39. Mfg'd by K&H Industries, available from C&H Distributors. Elfa Wire Baskets: Letter basket (top), $11.00; waste basket (below), $16.00. Scan Plast.

It's tempting to omit the fact that we found this coat rack a bit difficult to assemble, but in the words of a certain ex-president, it would be wrong. So if this kind of frustration reduces you to tears, we suggest you avoid it. If you do choose to order it, your patience will be well rewarded with an item that's an instant closet. If you want to screen it off, we suggest using a venetian blind installed on the ceiling some 3 feet from the wall. The instrument stand may never be the cosiest object you own, but with casters and an adjustable clamp-on tray, it may be one of the most useful.

*Valet II Coat Rack: Steel frame and shelves, chrome hanger bar, nylon umbrella holders, baked enamel finish in gray, beige, tan, bronze, putty or black, $98.00. American Hotel Register. **Mayo Instrument Stand:** Chrome legs, stainless steel tray, tripod caster base, tray height adjusts 34–43", $65.60, shown with extra clamp-on tray ($20.00 additional). Arista Surgical Supply. **Ashtray:** Steel, red finish, white lettering "Smokers Help Prevent Fires," $8.90. Crown Discount.*

You won't want to buy this just to have a cute platform for a plant or an ashtray, but if you're looking for a really solid swing-out tray, this is it. It will come in handy at bedside, but you might well have other places in mind.

Dental Tray Wall Mount: Aluminum arms, 33" maximum extension, stainless steel tray (9" × 14"), $58.40. Arista Surgical Supply. (Single- and double-arm units in addition to the three-arm unit shown here, are available for less.)

If there are any people who actually like the endlessly similar floral patterns which adorn most tissue boxes, they'll find this stainless steel dispenser somewhat beside the point.

Tissue Dispenser: Stainless steel, $7.39. American Hotel Register.

If you're in the early stages of an energy conservation crusade you might not be thrilled to see that these rolling tables come with electrical plug attachments. But if you're still wedded to such decadent objects as clock radios, lamps or even electric blankets you might even see their value as bedside tables. The locking casters may also not seem like an essential feature, but they make these stands perfect for use as a TV table.

Pixmobil Mobile Machine Stands: Baked enamel in beige or aquamarine, ribbed black rubber top pad, 4" casters, 24"l × 18"w × 17"h, $66.95. Electric plug mold attachment in red, $18.00 additional (add suffix "A"). Advance Products Co.

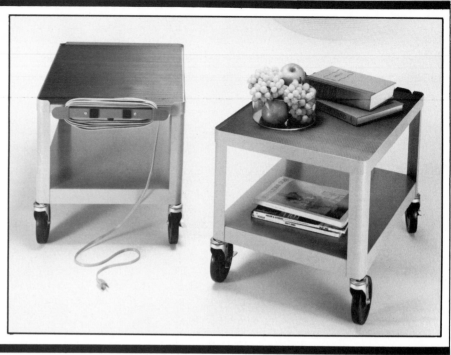

Garment Racks: (left to right) Chrome hanger rod and shelf, 32" length, $15.48. Chrome wall costumer, 22½" high, $7.98. Both from Crown Discount Corp.

We tend to think of clothes closets as being either large pieces of furniture or built-in fixtures that are some 3 or 4 feet deep and as tall as the room. There's nothing unreasonable about that, but it is limiting. Here, for example, is a simple lightweight unit that could serve as a second closet in a spare room or even an unused corner—and it's neither furniture nor built-in. On the right is a unit that holds coats every bit as efficiently as a coat stand, despite the fact that it doesn't have the familiar shape.

A compact but uncrowded bedroom office. The desk's high and gently sloped surface is comfortable to use in both a sitting and standing position. If the flip-top school desk compartment brings back unpleasant memories, paint the desk to banish any institutional associations and enjoy the extra storage space for what it is. The drafting chair is well suited to this setup, both by virtue of its height and looks, and the same could be said of the photography light.

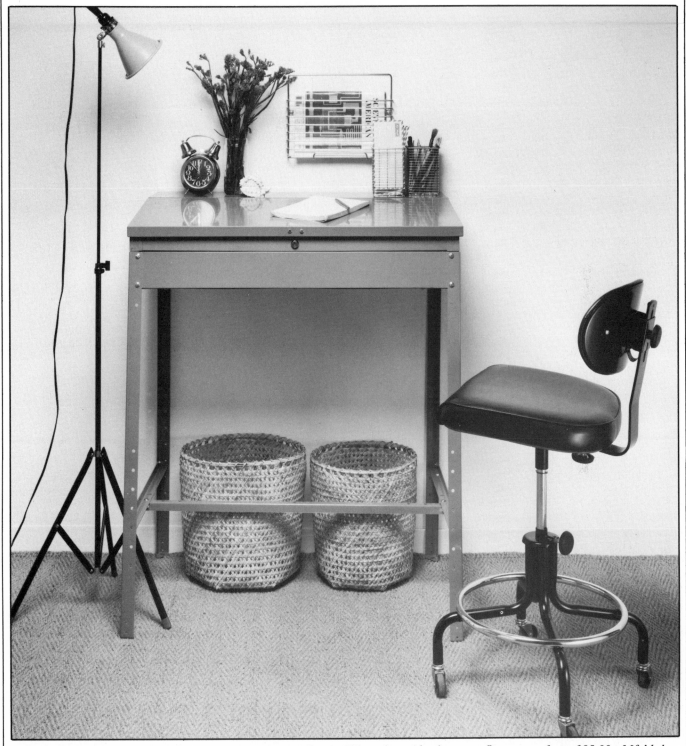

Hallco Shop Desk: Steel, gray, 36 1/2"w × 24 1/2"d × 43"h, adjustable footrest, flip-top surface, $95.00. Mfg'd by Hallowell, available from Lloyd Engineering Co. *Medical Chart Holder:* Polished chrome, 13 1/2"w × 10 1/2"h × 1 1/2"d, $44.50. Peter Pepper Products. *Photography Light:* Steel light stand, black, adjusts 42–78"; aluminum reflector, 5" diameter, in red, yellow, green, brown, blue or white, $36.00. Smith Victor. *Drafting Chair:* Steel frame, baked enamel finish in black or gray, vinyl seat (black or green), height adjusts 20–26", $82.50. Charrette's. *Coco Matting:* One-sided herringbone pattern, tan, $1.17 square foot, Import Specialists.

It's not all that surprising to find that an industry which markets "boutique collections" of Kleenex also produces a range of decorator products for the bathroom. Recently, however, whole stores devoted to bathroom supplies have become commonplace. Most of them are, predictably enough, filled with the kind of gimmicky, cute items which have only a distant relationship to their intended use.

Yet this is an area in which

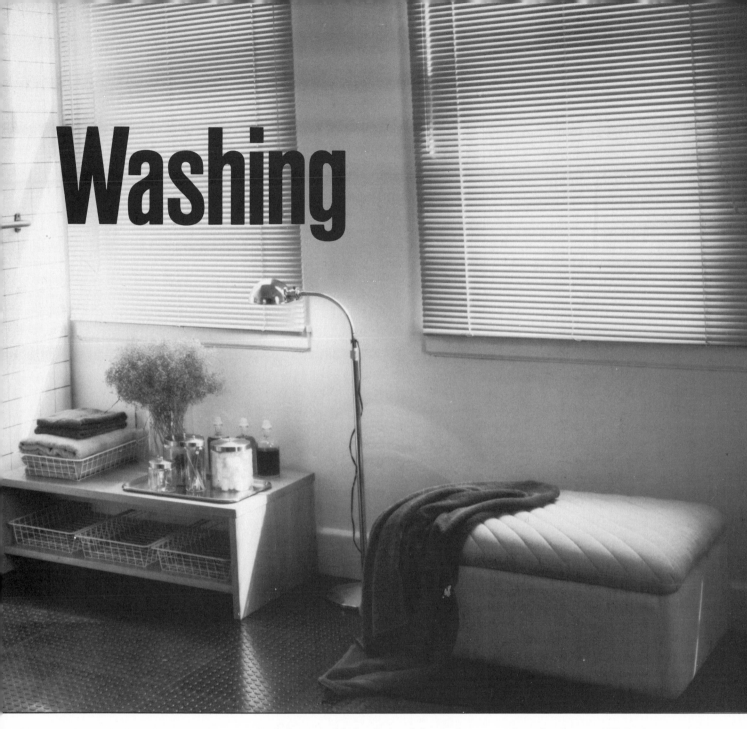

Washing

form ought to follow function in the simplest way. Madison Avenue may change the look of soap boxes and toilet paper displays every year, but these changes have little impact on the way we shower or arrange our bathrooms.

Think about the way in which the bathroom differs from other rooms: it's a place where you have a need for good lighting but is usually visually cold to start off with—which tells you something about what kind of lighting to think about; it's used by different members of the family and is therefore more likely to become messy and chaotic (finding good storage requires less effort than endless nagging); and it's generally a fairly small room, which means that you need to be aware of space.

These considerations may seem too obvious to bother with, but if you just head for the first objects that strike your fancy without having first considered these basics, you'll find you might as well have stayed with the boutique collections. That, to echo the introduction to this book, is the difference between decoration and design.

Multitier Locker: Steel, baked enamel finish in red, green, gray or tan. Each locker 12"w × 12"h × 12"d, approximately $85.00 per five-tier section (three shown). Mfg'd by Penco, available from C&H Distributors. (Single-, double- and triple-section combinations available.)

Bathrooms with storage space to spare are about as common these days as polar bears in the tropics. These lockers not only stand up to humidity and provide an abundance of storage space, but they break that space up into many small compartments. This way different family members can use and abuse their bathroom closet without interference from anyone else.

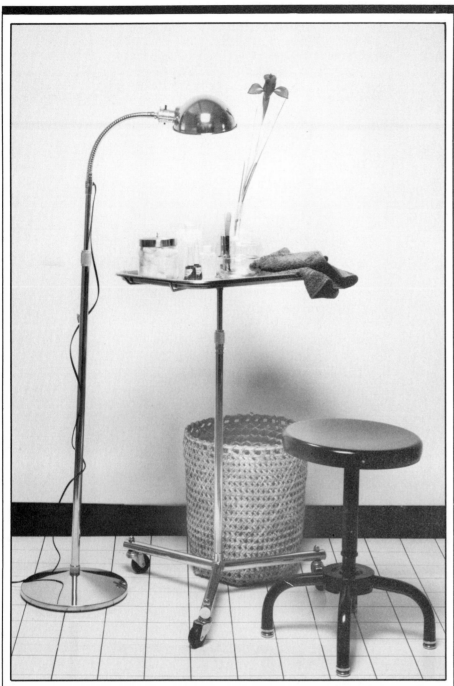

Instrument Stand: Chrome, stainless tray, tripod caster base, height adjusts 34–43", $65.50. Arista Surgical Supply. **Lab Stool:** *Baked enamel in black or gray, seat height adjusts 19–27", $49.14. Scientific Products.* **Standard Examining Lamp:** *Chrome, gooseneck head, height adjusts 54–73", $34.50. Arista Surgical Supply.*

Three objects of adjustable height, all made for doctors. A glance will tell you that each does what it's supposed to do with a minimum of fuss. The lamp's gooseneck enables you to tilt the light any way you care to, the stand is easily rolled around (though it's not designed for *heavy* loads) and the stool has a handsome and easily maintained enamel finish.

The Elfa baskets look just like they were designed in Sweden (and, in fact, they *were* designed in Sweden). The exception, in that it looks neither modern nor Scandinavian, is the wide bathtub basket which has ancestors dating back to the days when bathtubs had claws. Above it is its smaller cousin, the soap and brush basket.

Below them are the familiar bike baskets and the clean-looking dish drying rack, which makes a great shelf in any room. To the left, in and out trays are wall mounted for storage. The cart is composed of a simple but strong frame which will hold a variety of basket combinations. The frames themselves can be stacked one on top of the other. While the casters made for it are expensive, they're also really terrific—we just haven't seen better.

The glass top, by the way, is our addition. A piece this size costs about $8.00.

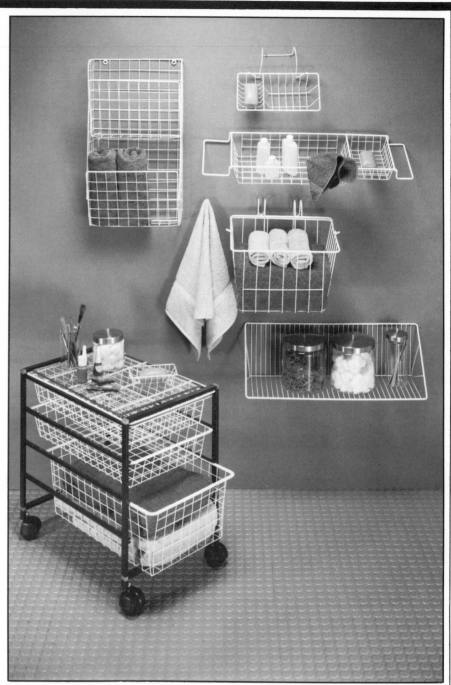

Elfa Wire Space-Gainer System: (front) All white, epoxy-coated wire baskets and metal cart frame in chocolate brown. (wall left) In and out tray, 21 1/4"h × 12 1/2"w, $19.00. (wall, top right) Soap and brush basket, 11 1/2"l × 6"w, $4.50. (wall right, second from top) Bathtub basket, 27 1/2"l × 8"d, $10.00. (wall, bottom right) Dish drying rack, 17 3/4"l, $13.50. (floor left) Cart frame, $30.00. Wheels, $21.50 set of four. (They're great if you need portability.) Shallow cart basket, $9.00. Deep cart basket, $10.50. (top of cart) Soap tidy, $3.00. All from Scan Plast.

Towel Supply Shelves: Stainless steel, 24"w × 8"d, (top) $25.65, (bottom) with towel bar, $32.90. Mfg'd by Lawson, both available from Beam Supply. (Also available in 18" width.)

These shelves from Beam Supply are prime examples of the kind of handsome, well-made and reasonably priced items which are just what you want and more than you can ever find. While you're being shown a badly made shelf with all new boutique scallop trim, these are just a phone call away.

The next time you're running out of bathroom closet space, remember that shelves like these can create storage space out of thin air.

There are places where the best decoration is no decoration at all, and this bathroom wall is one of them. Here an inexpensive and well-designed towel holder and an unadorned mirror and shelf unit look considerably smarter than fancier setups costing three times as much. A series of the towel holders, which you've probably seen in motels, not only holds a large family's supply, but looks terrific.

Channel Frame Mirror with Shelf: Stainless steel frame, 5" deep shelf, 16"w × 24"h, approximately $22.00. Accessory Specialties. (Also available in other sizes.) *Plaza Towel Holder:* Chrome, regular "four-guest" model, $8.40. American Hotel Register. *Vials:* Erlenmeyer Flasks, under $6.00. Arthur A. Thomas. *Culture Dishes:* Laboratory glass, $1.75 each. Arthur A. Thomas.

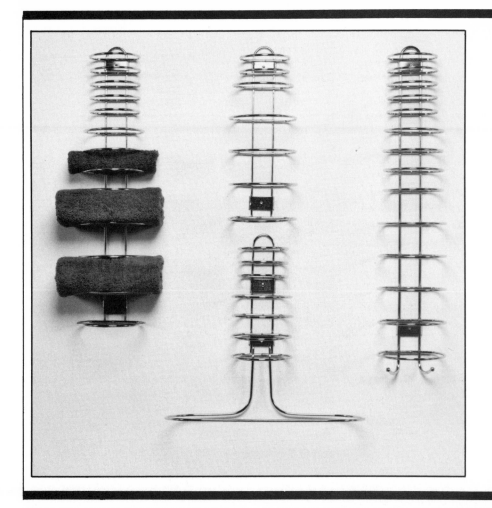

More towel holders, all designed by a motel owner. The towel bar on the center bottom holder is an attachment which comes in widths of 12 inches and 16 inches. The tall holder on the right has two hooks below its lowest rung. Both the towel bar and the hooks provide a place to hang unfolded towels.

Plaza Towel Holders: (left) 4-Guest Regular, chrome, $8.40. (center-top) 4-Guest Bath, $6.38. (center-bottom) 4-Guest Vanity, $6.38, shown with 16" towel bar attachment ($2.91 additional). (right) 4-Guest Valet, $9.52. All from American Hotel Register.

There is no clear logic to why these racks are made available for dentists' offices and not for our homes. They're wall mounted so they won't take up space, and in the bathroom they have obvious advantages over the floor. Somehow the pictures in *Life* just don't have the same impact when the pages are soggy and as rippled as crepe.

Literature Racks: Molded plastic, attach with magnets, screws, or pressure-sensitive tape, smoke (shown) or clear, 9¾" long (left), $6.50; 15½" long (right), $6.95. Temrex-Interstate Dental.

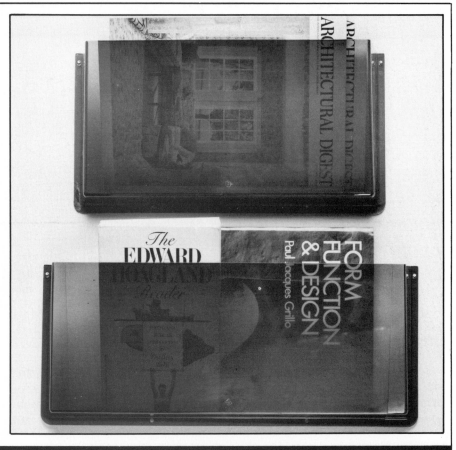

Ceniera Light: 10-3/4" diameter, surface mounted, etched glass with edges in white or red (shown), $35.00; chrome, $45.00; brass, $55.00. Thunder and Light. Surgical Dressing Jar: Glass, metal airtight top, 6" × 6", $5.50. Arista Surgical Supply. Graduated Beaker: 10-ounce size, approximately $1.55. Arthur H. Thomas.

The Ceniera light is large and handsome with its bright plastic frame, and large and handsome and just a bit more formal with a chrome or brass frame ($10 and $20 more respectively). The surgical dressing jar is obvious enough, but you may not have noticed that the water glass is a graduated lab glass beaker.

You may keep pencils in an old cigar box, but professionals who require a slightly higher level of organization often use a rotating tray like the model shown above. Make-up is only one alternative use, but it serves to show off the tray's ability to store many small objects in such a way that they can be easily found. A cigar box is "small storage" and laying objects out on a table top makes them easy to find—but it's the combination of these two properties that's harder to achieve.

The enamel tissue dispenser can also be wall mounted, and the extension mirror comes in both standard and magnifying versions.

Rotating Tray: Plastic, 10" diameter, black, white, orange or yellow, $14.25. Charrette's. Tissue Dispenser: White enamel, wall-mountable, $5.54. American Hotel Register. Extension Mirror: Chrome, standard and magnifying, 8" wide, extends 30", $26.85. Brookstone. Flat-Bottomed Round Flask: Laboratory glass, 1 liter, $9.70. Arthur H. Thomas.

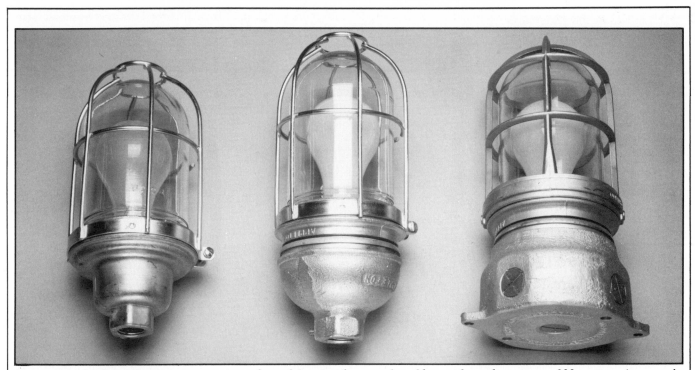

Vaporating Lights: Aluminum mounting, glass globes in clear, amber, blue, red, opal or green, 100 watts, wire guard. (left to right) Ceiling mount, $53.00. Pendant mount, $49.30. Wall mount, $34.50. Appleton Electric.

If we didn't think these vaportight lights were beautiful we wouldn't bother with them. They look tricky to install, and they are—we strongly suggest you let your local electrician do it for you. They're well suited for humid places like bathrooms, but good-looking enough—particularly in a series—for almost anywhere.

Not that many magazine racks would look right in a bathroom, but this medical chart holder is one of the few that do. The toilet paper holder and shelf above it may not be as elegant, but are certainly no less practical. The ashtray is designed with easy maintenance in mind. Neither of them is cheap, but both seem well worth knowing about.

Toilet Paper Holder and Shelf with Recessed Ashtray: Aluminum, 18" length, approximately $34.00. Accessory Specialties. (Also available with double roll.) Medical Chart Holder: Polished chrome, 13 1/2"w × 10 1/2"h × 1 1/2"d, $44.50. Peter Pepper Products.

You're looking at two objects designed to hold glasses and bottles upright on a swaying boat. They're quite inexpensive and, we think, extremely attractive as well. On the left is a holder with two elements—we've shown the mounted ring alone and with a cup. On the right are two identical holders which can be used with a glass as shown, but will also hold mouthwash bottles and the like.

Swinging Glass Holder in Gimbals: (left) Brass, chrome plated, 1 3/4" round, $4.95. Manhattan Marine. Gimbaled Glass, Can, Mug and Bottle Holder: (right) Stainless steel wire, $6.50. Manhattan Marine.

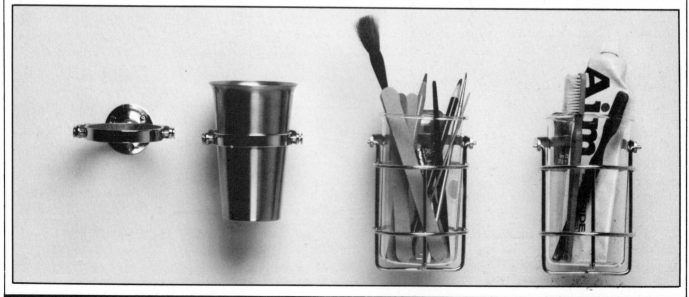

Soap Dishes: (from top, clockwise) #2213, brass, $18.60. #1213, stainless steel, $20.60. #4411, forged brass with liner, $14.20. All from Charles Parker Co. Soap dish with washcloth bar, $13.25. Accessory Specialties.

And you thought a soap dish was just a soap dish. The dish at top center is made of forged brass, while the one at top right is of stainless steel, but the two are similar in design and in simple good looks. The lower dish has the desirable and all too rare property of appearing infinitely more pricey than it is. (Though we should add that none of these is particularly cheap.)

And if you've ever stood in the bathroom, washcloth in one hand and soap in the other, thinking, "Gosh! If only they made something to hold both," the Accessory Specialties people have something to show you.

It's usually trash which is dropped through these familiar swing doors, but that's only because most of us have never thought to use these containers for anything else. The four above range from breadbox size to over 3 feet tall, and can be used to hold laundry, baseball bats, hardware supplies and practically anything else—including trash.

For what it's worth, the one at the back left is our favorite—so tall, so clean, such dignity of bearing!

Steel Receptacles: Baked enamel in white, green or gray, (clockwise from right front) 9" × 9" × 10", $20.60. 11 1/2" × 11 1/2" × 24 1/2", $49.45. 11 1/2" × 11 1/2" × 41 1/2", $57.29. 16 1/2" × 16 1/2" × 37", $60.98. All from American Hotel Register.

Dome Top Waste Receptacle: Baked enamel finish in red, white, green or beige, 15-gallon capacity, with galvanized rubber or plastic liner (recommended), $62.30. Mfg'd by United Metal, available from Beam Supply. (Other sizes and chrome finish available.) Elevated Basket: Steel runners, casters, nylon basket in red, green, yellow, blue and other colors, 2-bushel capacity, $26.85. Steele Canvas Basket Co. (Available in capacities of 1–6 bushels, and with basket in white canvas.)

These two objects, because they're so simple, adapt effortlessly to other uses. Here the familiar streamlined waste receptacle and an elevated basket are being used as laundry hampers. The design of the dome top receptacle is a perfectly straightforward expression of its function. The basket is also hard to beat—it's not only light, strong and mobile, but it has a bin raised to a non-back-breaking height.

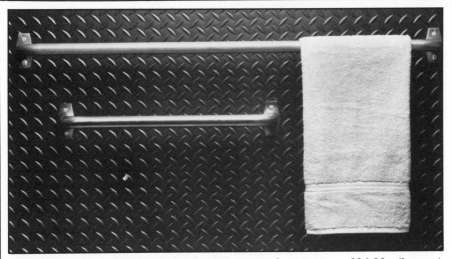

Grab bars are exactly what they sound like—bars which when mounted to the wall can be grabbed for support. Youve probably seen them in hospital hallways and bathrooms, but as strength is not your primary consideration—you are, after all, only hanging towels on them— you should order them in the thinnest diameter (listed as O.D.) and lightest gauge metal.

Grab Bars: (top) Diamond finish, 36" exposed mounting, $26.00. (bottom) Smooth finish, 18", exposed mounting, $19.50. Both from Accessory Specialties. (Other sizes and configurations, as well as concealed mountings, are available.)

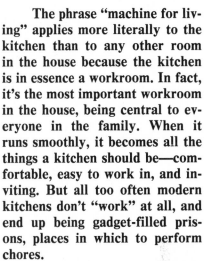

Food

The phrase "machine for living" applies more literally to the kitchen than to any other room in the house because the kitchen is in essence a workroom. In fact, it's the most important workroom in the house, being central to everyone in the family. When it runs smoothly, it becomes all the things a kitchen should be—comfortable, easy to work in, and inviting. But all too often modern kitchens don't "work" at all, and end up being gadget-filled prisons, places in which to perform chores.

If the kitchen is a machine, the main functions of the machine are related to food: storage of food and cooking materials, and preparation, which covers everything from slicing bread to baking casseroles. Any kitchen, then, must first of all be designed to perform its functions. So before you replace a single gadget you need to look at the basic design of your kitchen—which simply means seeing how the layout of the room serves the people who use it.

You don't need a university course to train you to "think like a designer." You simply need to have your eyes opened to new possibilities. For example, while you may look at your kitchen with its two closets and conclude that there is no storage space, a designer will see potential storage areas on every square foot of surface—on the ceiling, on an unused section of the wall, or in the "dead space" behind the door. And a designer familiar with industrial products will know that there are alternatives to custom-made carpentry fixtures or gimmicky and expensive storage systems.

Wall Storage Cabinet: Steel, gray baked enamel finish, 30"h × 30"w × 12"d, two shelves, steel pegboard doors, $49.97. Mfg'd by Homak, available from C&H Distributors. Reverse-Top Work-Storage Cabinet: Steel, baked enamel, gray, 24"l × 24"w × 34"h, two shelves (one adjustable), steel top reversible with 2" lip, $87.77. Mfg'd by Edsal, available from C&H Distributors. (Casters, $11.13 additional.)

The wall cabinet is about the same price as the tin cupboards you see in the housewares department. The big difference is that there is nothing remotely flimsy about this one, as we discuss more fully on page 114.

The rolling cabinet is also extremely sturdy and it has the advantage of providing both storage space and a mobile work surface (see page 31). These are exactly the sort of objects which would be well worth the trouble to paint.

The Pixmobile is a cart on wheels, but it has a number of features which make it a particularly useful one. Firstly, it has large casters and a strong frame, which means it's practical for large, heavy appliances. Secondly, it has an add-on plug mold, so your food warmer, coffee maker or whatever can be plugged right into the cart.

The third feature is less obvious but no less pleasing—the top is fitted with a ribbed rubber mat which prevents dishes or glasses from slipping while being rolled from kitchen to the table.

We've shown two possible ways to use them. The one on the left—at work height—we've considered a food preparation stand, while its lower and somewhat sleeker companion stands ready to serve.

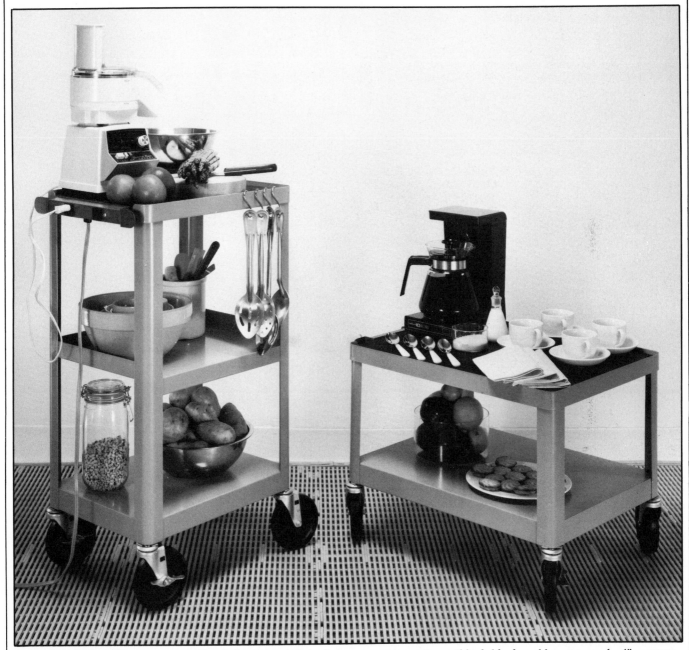

Pixmobile Mobile Machine Stands: Baked enamel in beige or aquamarine, ribbed black rubber top pad, 4" casters. (left) Model AV431, 18"l × 14"w × 32"h, $68.95. (right) Model AV447, 24"l × 18"w × 17"h, 12" from bottom to top shelf, $66.95. Electrical plug mold in red, $18.00 additional (add suffix "A"). All from Advance Products Co.

The pots and pans hanging against the wall are suspended from S-hooks on a Stanley's Closet Pole Bracket (a steal at $3.85). We used a plain mop handle and you can use a simple arrangement such as cup hooks screwed into a shelf for even more storage. The generously proportioned worktable supplies an invaluable commodity—a large surface to work on—and the rolling cart moves around. Now it's true that lots of things do that, but do they carry things from table to oven, from kitchen to dinner table? Do they have a drawer, and two large shelves?

Never underestimate the power of an object on casters.

Stationary Workbench: Steel in red or gray baked enamel, 48"l × 29"d × 34"h, $99.65. Shure Mfg. (Available in other sizes, with industrial butcher block tops, and/or casters.) Scotty Cart: Steel, baked enamel in red or gray, 3" casters, drawer, $88.35. Extra shelf (shown), $13.45. Shure Mfg. Stanley's Combination Shelf and Closet Pole Bracket: Chrome or white brackets, $3.85. Stanley Mfg. (Available at most hardware stores.)

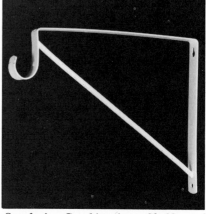

Stanley's Combination Shelf and Closet Pole Bracket: Bright steel or white, holds shelf and closet pole, $3.85 a pair. Stanley Mfg. (Available at most hardware stores.)

The main components in this compact work area are the wall-mounted—and therefore extremely sturdy—workbench, Sun Glo's oak adjustable-height stool and the handsome deep dome RLM light. The most familiar object here is probably the enamel bullet-shaped waste can. It's not cheap, but it's large and bright and one of those designs it's almost impossible to imagine improving.

Wall-Mounted Workbench: Steel, baked enamel finish in gray or red, 48"l × 29"d × 34"h, $85.10. Shure Mfg. (Other sizes available, also with industrial butcher block tops.) **Sun Glo Stool:** *Solid oak turn stool, height adjusts 24–30", $50.00. Sun Glo. (Also available 18–24", $45.00.)* **Dome Top Waste Receptacle:** *Baked enamel finish in red, white, beige, green or chrome (extra), 15 gallons, $62.30. Beam Supply.* **Deep Dome RLM:** *Porcelain enamel, white, red, yellow, green, etc., 20" diameter, $53.00. Abolite.* **Coffee Flag:** *Nylon marine flag, 18"l × 12"w, $6.25. Manhattan Marine.*

Wood Stools: Solid oak turn stools, adjustable heights, 18–24", $45.00; 24–30", $50.00. Sun Glo Corp.

We wanted to show you, without wandering too far afield, that the search for the functional can lead you in unexpected directions. These are hand-crafted stools made by a small company in New York State—not your typical industrial supplier—and you could hardly wish for a simpler or more efficient adjustable seat. The smaller one is ideal for kids, the larger for a bar or high counter stool.

A preparation area that could just as easily serve as a home office. The workbench is made from components: steel legs, steel shelf and bonded wood table top. We got a little carried away with the top, but you don't have to: a 1-inch thick composition board (often called "chip board") top from a lumber yard will cost only about $20.00, and be virtually every bit as good.

Utensils hang on an Elfa hall rack, and other Elfa baskets hold fruit, jars and so on. We were indulgent about Siegel's fabulous juicer (left) (see page 92) which wins hands down over all the electrics, but we tried to redeem ourselves with Charrette's dead simple, and dead cheap, Royalmetal chair.

Workbench from Components: Bonded wood top, 1 3/4 " thick, 5'l × 30"w, $97.56. Steel legs, 28 1/2 "d × 29"h, gray or colors, $21.44 a pair. Shelf, 5' long, steel in gray or colors, $18.27 additional. All from Equipto. Royalmetal Chair: Steel, masonite seat inset, height adjusts 24–32", $29.39. Charrette's. Standard Dome RLM: Porcelain-on-enamel, green, white, blue, red, black or yellow, 14" diameter, up to 150 watts, approximately $35.00. Abolite. (Wire guard available and 16" or 18" diameters available). Elfa Baskets: Epoxy-coated white wire. Hall racks (utensils), 19 3/4 "w, $13.00; glassholders (right, front), 12 1/2 "w, $3.00; basket unit, 25 1/4 "h, $20.00. All from Scan Plast.

If $30.00 seems like a lot to pay for a scale, consider that this one not only mounts anywhere, has a weighing pan which folds down for use (and is removable for cleaning), but looks like a million dollars. The pan slides out effortlessly, which makes the process of measuring a whole lot easier, and the scale is graded in both grams and ounces.

Wall Scale: 8 3/4 " diameter, folds against wall, reads to 6 pounds 10 ounces, $34.24. Brookstone.

What's cheaper than butcher block, easier on your knees than marble, practically indestructible, easy to clean and a doctor-recommended ingredient twice as effective as aspirin?

The answer is Saniblock (we lied about the last part), which is said to be *the* new cutting block in the restaurant trade.

Saniblock: High-density polyethylene, buff colored, 18" × 12", $17.07. U.S. Mat and Rubber.

*Food Preparation Island: Slotted angle, red enamel finish, 6'h × 36"w × 24"d, three steel shelves in red baked enamel finish, $84.38, 5" casters, $35.80 set of four (shown). Equipto. **Laboratory Stool:** Steel base, footrest, foam seat, gray or beige enamel finish, $64.78. Mfg'd by Ajusto, Scientific Products. **Dome Top Waste Receptacle:** Baked enamel finish in red, white, green or beige, galvanized or plastic liner (recommended), 15 gallons, $62.30. Mfg'd. by United Metal, available from Beam Supply. (Other sizes and chrome finish available.) For information about professional cookware, see pages 92, 93.*

We had the Equipto Company make this up from our design to show you that all our talk of slotted angle (page 28) and steel shelving (page 18) was worth the time and trouble.

The bright red frame supports a work surface and two shelves. S-hooks through the perforations in the slotted angle provide almost limitless hanging space on any part of the frame.

We don't think casters proved to be particularly well suited to this object, and we suggest that if you order it from Equipto, who is now shipping it as an unassembled unit, you skip them.

But even with the casters it stands as an example of what can be done with slotted angle when it's used imaginatively.

The only question we have about these test tube baskets is how we've managed to live without them all these years. They're good-looking and practical, and just look at those prices!

Test Tube Baskets: Rectangular baskets, $5.56; round baskets, between $7.40 and $12.43. All from Arthur H. Thomas.

Maid's Baskets: (left to right) Perforated steel, rubber feet, 17 1/2"l × 9 1/2"w × 4"h, three compartments, $10.64. Aluminum, 20"l × 10 3/8"w × 4 3/4"h, three compartments, $12.26. Both from American Hotel Register.

These are maid's baskets, and we can't say enough about them. They're cheap, strong and very light, and as they say on Madison Avenue, they've got a hundred and one uses. Apart from using them to carry stuff outdoors for barbecues and the like, you can also use the perforated model to hold silverware for drying.

Cart: Steel, gray enamel, 5" casters, 30"l × 16"w × 32"h, two shelves, $42.77. Extra shelf: (shown) 3" lip, $9.34. Drawer (not shown), $9.96. Mfg'd by Edsal, available from C&H Distributors.

It all looks very professional and gourmet-chef-like, but it's just a very inexpensive utility cart taken out of the warehouse and put into the kitchen. Thanks to that miracle of human ingenuity, the S-hook, utensils hang within easy reach. The top can be fitted with butcher block which, if not really thick, should be placed on wood spacers to make it a touch higher than the sides of the tray. The trays can also be reversed (lips down) and a drawer is also available. Consider the possibilities.

Made to be used as drafting stools, these seats have a finish that will withstand almost anything you care to spill on them. As with the other pairs, the smaller of the two (24 inches high) is ideal for use while sitting at a table, while the 30-inch model is better suited for counter work.

Wood Drafting Stools: (right) Birch, varnish finish, 24" high, $44.10; (left) 30" high, $51.90. Both available from Charrette's.

The Magnabar is now a familiar object in many kitchens, or rather, a version of the magnetized knife holder is. This, from Arista Surgical Supply, costs about the same as the imitations, and it's much stronger.

Magnabar: 18" magnetic tool holder, $11.50. Arista Surgical Supply.

Workbench: Bonded wood top, 5'l × 30"w × 1 3/4" thick, $97.56. Bench legs, 34 1/2"h × 29"w, $22.57 (per pair). 5' steel shelf, $18.27. All from Equipto. **Lab "Clean Room" Chair:** *Steel base, polystyrene swivel seat with wood grain molded surface, adjustable back, height adjusts 17–25", $78.90. Ajusto.* **"Smokers Prevent Fires" Ashtray:** *Metal in red, $5.82. Mfg'd by Kier, available from C&H Distributors.* **Clock:** *Aluminum housing in white, black face (also chrome and colors), 10" diameter, battery, electric or quartz operated, $54.50. Peter Pepper Products.* **Radial Wave RLM:** *Porcelain enamel, black or white, 20" diameter, $54.00. Abolite.*

Equipto's worktable can also be ordered with steel, masonite and steel, bonded wood, and laminated maple tops. They come in a variety of widths and depths, with drawers and more than one kind of shelf. There is yet another, much cheaper alternative: going to the nearest lumberyard for a composition board top.

This model has a single shelf, holding the cookware, and a pressed wood top. The Rolodex holds recipes (see page 97), the clock tells the time (handsomely, if expensively), and the Ajusto "clean room" chair just looks gorgeous (if you had a shiny stainless steel base and an adjustable back and seat you would too). Two radial wave RLM lights float elegantly above the whole thing, and we just included the sandbox ashtray to bring us all back to earth.

This fold-up nurse's desk seems to us to be a giant step up from magnets on the refrigerator or thumbtacks in the wall. It folds flat (as shown) and opens to provide space for mail, recipes and so on, as well as a surface for writing or for holding open cookbooks.

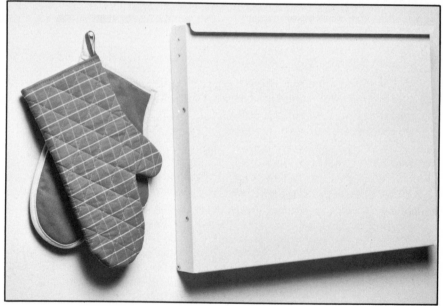

Nurse's Fold-Away Desk: Steel surface, 16" × 20.", back pocket sections, green, beige, white, walnut, $43.56. Mfg'd by Budget Buddy Company, C&H Distributors.

Bench: Wood, lacquered surface, 4' × 9 1/2", $41.62. Stable pedestals, 17 1/2" high, metal, @ $14.57. C&H Distributors.

Direct from the locker room, these benches offer an alternative for seating in large groups at the kitchen table. Available in 4-, 6-, 8-, 10-, or 12-foot smooth tops. And, as they're sturdy and low, they're terrific for kids.

The Elfa basket on the right is simple enough—typical of the system's clean and well-proportioned designs. The two baskets and shelf arrangement of the unit on the left is an endlessly useful item, one which could as easily be used in a bathroom or workroom or storage area. But they're both great on the kitchen because, apart from anything else, they won't collect dust.

Elfa Wire Baskets: White epoxy-coated wire (left) basket unit, 25 1/4"h, $20.00; (right) waste paper basket, 25 3/4"h, $28.00. Both from Scan Plast.

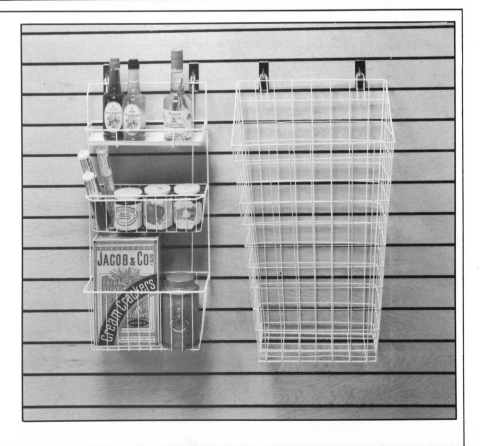

Multitier Locker: Steel, baked enamel finish in red, green, tan or gray. Single unit, five-boxes high, 12"w × 12"h × 12"d, approximately $85.00. Mfg'd by Penco, available from C&H Distributors.   (Three-locker-width units shown here. Other sizes available.) *Safety Ladder:* Two-step steel footstool, with spring-loaded casters, $73.66. Scientific Products.

The multiple-tier box locker works in the kitchen for the same reasons it works in the locker room—it provides many individual storage compartments without taking up much space. The boxes come in three different widths and depths, and can be ordered in units five or six tiers high and one, two or three lockers wide. We've shown the lockers with a safety ladder. It has spring-loaded casters and metal, nonskid steps, two features which, like so many things in life, don't sound that impressive but can make themselves felt by their absence. That nonskid surface, by the way, is designed for tougher material than the soles of your bare feet—you should only use it when wearing shoes.

Wine Bottle Rack: Metal frame (#7404), chocolate brown, $30.00 Shoe rack, epoxy-coated wire, $8.00 each. Mfg'd by Elfa, available from Scan Plast. Instrument Tray: Stainless steel, 13 1/2" × 9 3/4", $9.50. Arista Surgical Supply.

To answer the question "Isn't there a shoe rack which can be converted to hold wine by reversing the racks?"—yes, and this is it, although to be absolutely accurate it's the other way around (for those who keep track of these things).

This is but one of the many possible combination of baskets which will fit the Elfa brown steel frame. The frame comes with terrific casters, but more about that later. Two or more frames can not only be stacked, but lock together to form a single column.

Elfa Storage Unit: Metal frame in chocolate brown (#7404 shown), $30.00. Bottom basket (#042), 7 1/4"h, $10.50. Top Baskets (#041), 3 3/8"h, @ $9.00. All from Scan Plast.

Lab glass is commonly found, unsurprisingly enough, in laboratories. The term encompasses an entire world of glass pieces which are available in an exhausting array of shapes, sizes, heights and styles. It's mostly inexpensive and heat-resistant and the fact that it's often striking and attractive is no longer big news.

Lab glass appears in various places throughout the book, but we assembled representatives of the main types to have as a reference.

Group (1) test tubes in S-shaped racks have write-on labels and screw-tops (cork tops are also available) and make great spice racks.

Group (2) surgical dressing jars are airtight and will keep almost anything fresh, but the storage jar (3) is not, despite the fact that we put cookies in it. The mortar and pestle (4) is beautiful and startlingly cheap, and the Erlenmeyer flasks (5) are but two of a family of flasks, all of which can be chilled and heated. The crystallizing dishes (6), thin, strong and good-looking, make great fruit or salad bowls, and the tall hydrometer cylinder (7) can be used for storage, but makes an unusual, slender vase. The large battery jar (8) is an-

other fragile-looking but sturdy object, and the same could be said of the flat-bottomed round flask (9) which happens to be perfectly shaped for use as a bud vase. The three Aquaria bowls (10) aren't quite so clearly named: look for them under "Animal Feeding Dishes" in the lab glass catalog. The volumetric flasks (11) are a little pricey, but they're also more graceful than most of the other pieces. The specimen jars (12) have close-fitting tops, and the wide-mouthed amber bottles (13) are as cheap, and as airtight, as anything you'll ever find.

(1) Test Tube Racks: 24 holes, metal, $8.72. Arthur H. Thomas. Screw Cap Test Tubes: smaller, $10.56 per dozen; larger, $10.85 per dozen. Arthur H. Thomas. (2) Surgical Dressing Jars: 3" × 3", $4.00; 4" × 4", $4.50; 5" × 5", $5.00; 6" × 6", $5.50. Arista Surgical Supply. (3) Storage Jars: soda lime glass, loose-fitting lid, 1 gallon, $4.80. Arthur H. Thomas. (4) Mortar and Pestle: glass, 16 ounces, $7.33. Arthur H. Thomas. (5) Erlenmeyer Wide Mouth Flask: cork top, 2 1/2 quart, $12.24. Erlenmeyer Graduated Flask: 1 quart, $12.97. Arthur H. Thomas. (6) Crystallizing Dishes: 8 1/2" diameter, $10.70; 4" diameter, $3.39. Both available from Scientific Products and Arthur H. Thomas. (7) Hydrometer Cylinder: 3" diameter, 18" high, $22.61. Arthur H. Thomas. (8) Battery Jar: 1 gallon, $5.75. Arthur H. Thomas. (9) Flat-Bottomed Round Flask: 1 quart, $9.70. Arthur H. Thomas. (10) Aquaria Bowls: 8" diameter, $5.50; 4 1/2" diameter, $2.50. Arthur H. Thomas and Scientific Products. (11) Volumetric Flask: 1 quart, $19.15; 2 quart, $24.19. Arthur H. Thomas. (12) Specimen Jars: flint glass, close-fitting tops, $1.75. (13) Wide-Mouthed Amber Bottles: 1 ounce, $5.45 per dozen; 2 ounce, $6.25 per dozen; 4 ounce, $7.80 per dozen; 8 ounce, $8.20 per dozen; 32 ounce, $12.80 per dozen. Arthur H. Thomas.

Akro-Mils Storage System: (top left) Louvered panel, steel in gray, 35 3/4"w × 19"h, $14.66. (bottom left) Bench rack, metal in gray, 27 1/2"l × 21"h, $24.78. (right) Akro-Bins, polypropylene, various sizes in red, yellow or blue, between $.55 and $6.97 each. All from C&H Distributors.

Akro-Mils bins are colorful plastic containers which have provided efficiently organized storage in factories and workshops for years. You'll just have to take our word for it when we tell you that these bins are bright yellow, red and blue. Bin sizes range from 3 inches by 4 1/8 inches all the way up to 14 3/4 inches by 16 1/2 inches by 7 inches. Prices range from $.55 to $6.97. These bins are widely adaptable: they stack vertically, nest inside one another, or hook onto the louvered panels, which come in wall-mounted (top left and right) and bench rack (left) versions.

There are many sources for Akro-Bins, but let the buyer beware: a number of retail outlets have adopted these bins and are selling them at ludicrously inflated prices. We strongly suggest you go direct to the distribution source—materials handling suppliers—for the best prices.

Walk Gate: Steel frame, steel chain-link mesh, 72"l × 36"w, $44.99. J.C. Penney. Wood Drafting Stool: Birch, varnish finish, 30" high, $51.90. Charrette's.

More often than not there's a way to steal a good idea and find your own ways to use it. Wall hanging systems, for example, do not *have* to be pegboard or wood slats or any of the variations thereof. We've used an ordinary chain-link gate from J.C. Penney to illustrate the point. In fact, the S-hook and chain-link mesh system even has an advantage over the others, in that it can also be hung from the ceiling (parallel to the floor) to create hanging storage in unused air space.

Slat Wall: Gumwood, 4' square sheets, horizontal grooves 3" on center, $25.60. Chrome L-hooks (like pegboard hooks), between $1.30 and $2.00 (by size). John Byron Displays Ltd.

Slat walls are used by department stores to display hanging merchandise. Pegboard performs the same function, but let's face it, it's just not as attractive. This horizontal slat wall is available in gumwood maple, white ash, red or white oak (all these woods require a sealant finish for kitchen use). It can also be special ordered with Formica, metallic and painted surfaces. But be advised: Gumwood and maple are by far the cheapest of the various finishes.

A wide variety of hooks are manufactured, which can accommodate all types of utensils and pots and pans.

Slat Wall: Gumwood, "square cut," 4' × 4" sheets, $2.60 per square foot. Chrome hooks range from $1.30 to $2.00. John Byron Displays Ltd.

This is a second version of slat wall. It's known as "square cut" and comes in gumwood, red oak, white ash and white oak. Beyond that the difference between the two types comes down to a matter of looks. If you have a large blank wall and want more "decor," this square-cut grid will liven it up, and the quieter lines of the other type will probably be preferable for an already busy-looking kitchen.

These are a few of the different hooks available for slat wall. At top is a single unit with seven hooks, while those below are individual hooks in various lengths.

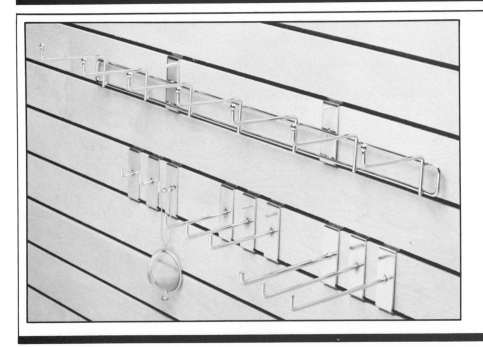

Slat Wall Hooks: (top) Bar with seven hooks, chrome, 26" long, $13.20. (bottom, left to right) Chrome hooks, 3/4", $1.30; 4", $1.40; 6", $1.60. All from John Byron Displays. (Other sizes, and zinc finish, also available.)

If you're gazing adoringly at the cookware in these and other photographs, we've made our point. We wanted to include just enough of the stuff to spark your interest. A whole world of professional quality cookware is out there, and it's not just for the professional chef. Huge restaurant ranges and sliding-door refrigerators cost a fortune—unless you get a great buy on used equipment—but many of these pots, pans and utensils don't. Even though they're a bit more than their counterparts in department stores, they will give you much more for your money, primarily because they'll last forever: they've been designed to survive incredible use and abuse.

The following items are a representative sampling of professional cookware.

In the photo on the left, the stainless steel mixing bowls in the front are $7.95 for the largest, $1.95 for the smallest. The cylindrical Bain Maries are $20 and

An Assortment of Professional Cookware and Utensils: Quiche pans (top left) from $1.10 to $4.00. Layer cake pans: (beneath) are $4.00 and less. Rolling pin is $11.00. The selection of stainless steel serving spoons (plain, perforated and slotted) are in the $3.00 range. Extra-large stainless steel funnel (hanging center) is $16.15. Ice tongs (right, hanging) are priced from $1.50 to $1.80. Tin mold (hanging, lower left) is $9.95. Porcelain Bain Maries (sitting, lower right with wood utensils) are $5.95 and $9.95. Selection of wooden utensils (in Bain Maries) runs from a little over $1.00 to about $8.50 for the extra-large wooden spoon. Four Vollrath stainless steel Bain Marie pots (sitting, back left), from $7.95 to $19.95. Tidynal Napkin Holder (front left), $6.95. Sugar dispenser (to right of napkin holder) is $1.50. Stainless steel mixing bowls (front center) between $1.95 and $13.95. Jiffy glass washer with double brushes and suction cup for sink base (far right) is $9.95. Siegel juicer (bottom center), $86.95. All from Daroma Restaurant Equipment.

less, and can be used for refrigerator storage, mixing or even as ice buckets. To the right of the juicer are their porcelain counterparts, $9.95 and $5.95 respectively.

The cookware in the photo on the right looks expensive and is, but it's a long way from Woolworth's. The dark Calphalon set (front right), for example, is made of specially treated heavy gauge aluminum alloys which won't chip, peel or age in any way, and have cast iron handles.

Almost every city large enough to have more than two lunch counters will also have a distributor of professional cookware. You can also order by mail (see Access section), but however you do it, remember that some of the items are going to be more than you need because of health codes that have no bearing on home use. Let common sense, and your local distributor, be your guides.

Calphalon: (dark gray pots and pans, lower right) Aluminum alloys, heavy gauge, cast iron handles. Saucepans between $24.30 and $49.25. Frying pans from $13.40 (7") up to $39.05 (14"). Stock pots (not shown) also available. Professional Kitchen. Paderno: (hanging, bottom left) Stainless steel with aluminum bottom. Frying pans (not shown) from $19.70 to $37.50. Saucepans from $20.00 to $40.00. Stock pots, from $20.00 up to $70.00. Professional Kitchen. French Omelete Pans: (hanging, top right) Steel, $11.00 and $12.00. Professional Kitchen. Toroware: (frying pans, top left; pots, bottom left) Aluminum, heavy gauge. Saucepans from $10.95 (1/2 quart) to $21.95 (8 1/2 quarts). Frying pans from $8.95 to $23.95. Stock pots (not shown) also available. Mfg'd by Leyse, available from Daroma Restaurant Equipment.

Although you might want to acquire these glass holders because they're handsome and space-saving, you should also know that if your house were to suddenly turn on its side, your bottles would stay perfectly upright. (They're built for use on boats.)

Swinging Glass Holder in Gimbals: (left) Brass, chromium plated, 1 ¾ " round, $4.95. Manhattan Marine. Gimbaled Glass and Bottle Holder: (right) Stainless steel wire, $6.50. Manhattan Marine.

Bottle Openers: (left) Standard opener, unpolished nickel plating, $1.40. (center) Standard opener, polished chrome plating, $2.52. (right) Cap catcher, satin-chrome finish, $4.09. All from American Hotel Register.

For some reason bottle openers tend to disappear—you can somehow never find one even when it's right there where you left it. For the royal sum of $1.40 you can buy one which screws to a wall, and if you can't find the wall you should stop fooling around with bottles. Big spenders willing to go all the way up to $4.09 can buy the model on the upper right that catches the bottle caps.

Dixie Marathon Industrial Roll Towel Dispenser: Steel construction, white baked enamel finish, $34.10. Paper towel rolls, two-ply, white stock, unperforated, $2.15. Both from Crown Discount (Perforated also available.) **Globe Top Soap Dispenser:** *Chrome finish, plastic globe, 6 5/8" high, 16-ounce capacity, $7.28. American Hotel Register and Beam Supply. Coconut soap (for dispenser), about $3.60 per gallon. Soap is available from both.*

These are just two examples of dozens of readily available towel and soap dispensers. The paper towel dispenser on the left uses towels you'll need to order from a commercial papergoods supplier, but it will be worth the savings in the long run. In case you've been on another planet for the past few years, paper towels have become very expensive, and many of us are accustomed to whipping through half a roll at a shot. With this dispenser you have to turn a crank to get the towel and you'll probably use a lot less.

The soap dispenser will also save you money, particularly if you follow our suggestion to buy liquid soap at $3.60 a gallon. We also see no reason why you can't use it to dispense dish-washing liquid.

The Taylor thermometer has the oversized, pop art look of those inflatable bananas that some kids (and some adults) find so intriguing. The thermometer at least has obvious scientific value (as opposed to the banana) but we also recommend the Edmund Scientific Catalog. The catalog features quite a few items of interest to even the most unscientific among us.

Wall Thermometer: 2' high, off-white, enameled wood, indoor Fahrenheit/Celcius scale, $19.95. Edmund Scientific.

Rolodex® Economy Card File: Nickel-plated frame, dust cover, holds 500 3" × 5" cards, $21.50. Crown Discount.

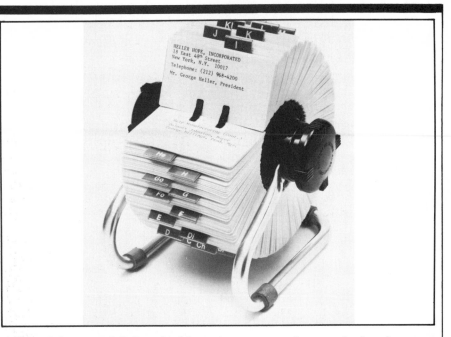

It may seem incongruous at first glance, but using a Rolodex® in the kitchen as a recipe file makes a great deal of sense. You don't necessarily have to go for the deluxe model, but the idea is the same with all three: cards can be easily located and lifted out for use. Plastic covers will protect your recipes from the fate every recipe card dreads more than any other—being defaced and rendered illegible by food stains.

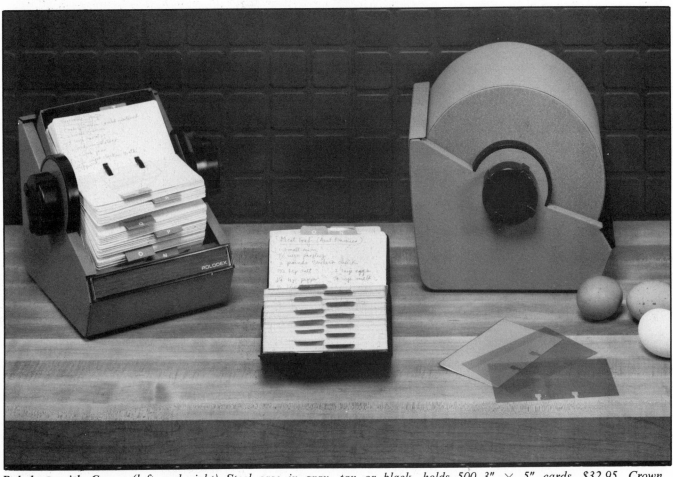

Rolodex® with Cover: (left and right) Steel case in gray, tan or black, holds 500 3" × 5" cards, $32.95. Crown Discount. Card Protectors: (lower right) Plastic in clear, orange, pink or yellow, box of 250, $22.50 (clear); $25.00 (colors). Crown Discount. (Smaller quantities available in stationery stores.) Rolodex® V-File Jr.: (center) Steel in gray, black or tan, holds 500 3" × 5" cards, $17.50. Crown Discount.

Lund Drawer Key Panel: Steel, gray, twenty-three key tags in green acetate, 11 3/4"w × 10"h, $13.20. Crown Discount.

What if someone appeared before you one morning as you were pinioned upside down behind the couch, looking for your lost keys in a panic-stricken frenzy, and said "Hey Mac, for thirteen bucks you'll never go through this again!"

You'd probably be surprised but intrigued. Here's what the $13 would buy you ($13.20 to be exact).

Grab Bars: (top) Stainless steel, knurled (grooved) finish, 36" long, $26.00. (bottom) Stainless steel, smooth finish, 18", $19.50. Both with exposed mountings. Accessory Specialties.

These hospital grab bars are an unlikely but practical hanging system, and a particularly flexible one at that. You can get them in different sizes and configurations that will mount in spaces too small for pegboard. Also available with sleeker, concealed mounting hardware.

Air-O-Mesh: Diamond-shaped mesh pattern, 24" wide rolls in clear, red, gray and green, about $2.00 per linear foot. Mfg'd by U.S. Mat & Rubber, available from local restaurant and hotel suppliers.

Air-O-Mesh is used in the sinks of many laboratories and institutional kitchens to reduce chipping and breakage as well as noise. It also happens to be a great idea for the shelves you keep cups and glasses on, because it allows air to circulate freely.

THE RLM

RLMs—the name sounds more interesting than it is, so we won't bore you—are porcelain-on-steel light reflectors that come in a handful of basic shapes and many different sizes. You've no doubt seen the knock-off versions in local housewares stores but we feel the real thing is generally worth the extra money (though it's by no means a rule that the imitations are always cheaper). They're well made and sturdy and have, pardon the phrase, a timeless elegance.

They're particularly good for general lighting as well as direct lighting over tables, though care has to be taken to avoid glare. Try low wattage, soft light bulbs or half-silvered bulbs which bounce light off the fixture dome. Half-silvered bulbs can be made from ordinary incandescents by spraying the bottom of the bulb with aluminum spray paint (though you must never cover more than half the rounded belly of the bulb or the filament will melt). To apply the spray, mask the top half of the bulb with tape and apply light, even coats.

Abolite makes a series of colored RLMs, though most are only available in white.

A few other points: Most of the big reflectors will come with "mogul" sockets, which will need a $3.00 to $5.00 adapter for bulbs under 200 watts. Ask a good electrical supply house for a mogul to medium socket base adapter. The heavier reflectors, such as the group on the left, should be hung on conduit (metal pipes) and *not* suspended from electrical cords. It's also a good idea to hang wire-hung lights in such a way that they're adjustable, to enable you to find the right height after installation.

Unless you're experienced you'll need an electrician for these. Also note that prices here are for shades only. An electrical supplier will have the additional parts, namely a "strain relief", about $.60 (a metal clip which goes around the wire to hold the weight of the fixture); the wire itself, sometimes called S-cord, about $.60/foot (183SVT for grounded, 182SVT for ungrounded), generally available in black and white; a canopy, about $1.50 (a small junction box which mounts on the ceiling and which will hold the wire or conduit); and conduit (for the larger fixtures).

The basic range of RLM shapes are arrayed on these pages along with other close relations. The aptly named standard dome (7) is the most common and most imitated shape. We're showing it with an optional wire guard, a good idea in kids' rooms. The shallow dome (1) shown here is fitted with a second guard, deeper but naturally similar. The elliptical angle reflector next to it (2) is less common, and well shaped for throwing light back onto a wall or bookcase—you wouldn't

Shallow Dome Reflector: Porcelain, 150–200 watts, approximately $20.00. Deep wire guard, about $10.00. Benjamin-Thomas Industries. Elliptical Angle Reflector: Porcelain in white, 200–300 watts, about $40.00. Benjamin-Thomas Industries.

want it over a dining room table. It should be hung on a wire conduit to give you control of where the light is thrown. The two deep bowl reflectors (3, 5) are similar, but only one allows (3) light to shine upward. Smaller versions of the bowl are available.

The light between the two (4) is another deep bowl fixture—not, as far as we can figure it, strictly an RLM, but alike in most respects. We've also shown it with it's glass cover in place (6), held there by metal clips.

The radial wave (8) is perhaps the loveliest of the RLMs, and we had to restrain ourselves from finding a need for them in every second photograph.

Deep Dome RLMs: Porcelain-on-enamel, 20" diameter, yellow, black, red, green, blue, white or black, mogul base. (left) With uplight. Both about $53.00. Abolite (Decorator series). **Open Reflector:** *(center) Aluminum, 14" diameter, mogul base, about $29.00. Abolite.*

Enclosed Mercury Reflector with Glass Cover: Aluminum, 14" diameter, hinged heat- and impact-resistant glass cover, 175 watts, approximately $80.00. Abolite. (Available also in porcelain-on-enamel.)

Standard Dome RLM: Porcelain-on-enamel in white, green, blue, red, yellow or black, 14" diameter, about $35.00. Convex wire guard, about $5.50. Abolite. (Other sizes and other model wire guards also available.)

Radial Wave RLM: Porcelain-on-enamel in black or white, 20" diameter, about $55.00. Abolite.

How to Use Fluorescent Lights in the Home

We're accustomed to seeing fluorescent lights in places like laundromats and discount stores, and we tend to think of them as cold and unflattering. But they're much too energy efficient to dismiss, and they don't have to be harsh.

What one has to do is simply reduce the intensity and glare, and we offer you three ways of doing that. The first is simply to use the right bulb. We recommend *warm white* bulbs, which give off the softest light, and warn you away from *daylight* lamps, which sound fine but aren't at all what you want for home lighting.

Because fluorescents generate very little heat, you can safely cover them with special colored plastic sleeves. The sleeves will create—no surprises here—colored light in amber and other tones. They're available from electrical and theatrical lighting supply houses for about $2.00 per running foot.

A third technique for diminishing glare is putting a barrier between your eyes and the light. A strip of wood about a foot wide, suspended about a foot beneath a ceiling-mounted fixture will virtually eliminate glare. The light will bounce off the baffle and then bounce a much softer, indirect light off the ceiling. The baffle can be painted for a different colored light effect. Baffles can also be used when mounting fluorescents on walls or beneath cabinets.

Flourescents, by the way, are readily available in circles and U-shapes as well as the familiar rods. These can make interesting lighting arrangements when used as design elements, all under $5.00–20.00 a bulb. Some of the sexy stuff you've seen done expensively with neon can be done inexpensively with fluorescents (within obvious limits).

Bob Chair: Metal enamel frame in red, yellow or white, $29.00. Conran's.

The old basic folding chair is neither old nor basic anymore. Sometimes, only sometimes, improvements on standard designs are worth taking seriously. This example is undeniably as light and as compact as the original, and it's quite handsome. But what's most surprising is that it's not suddenly eight times the price of the plainer version. (Just three times the price. For the old-fashioned version, see page 106.)

Instrument Trays: Stainless steel, 13 ½" × 9 ¾", $9.50. Larger sizes $11.25, $17.95. All from Arista Surgical Supply. Pyrex Culture Flask: Lab glass, approximately 2 ½ quarts, $20.56. Arthur H. Thomas.

One doesn't associate the world of medicine with great values or great style, yet these quietly stunning trays come from a surgical supply company. They're stainless steel and all under $20.00. The red Mondo Tiles make a beautiful table top (see page 108), and the lab glass speaks, if not sings, for itself.

The classic director's chair in a marine version which we think is better built and less expensive than the others. The fabric is washable, but be warned: colors run, so wash them separately. This is not just for cleanliness but also keeps the seat and back nice and taut. Replacement covers in many colors are also readily available for about $8.00 a chair, so you can change the color of a whole set without great inconvenience or enormous expense.

"Admiral" Director's Chair: Wood frame, acrylic-coated walnut or white finish, 18-ounce cotton duck cover in white, green, red or blue, 18" height, about $45.00. Tucker Duck and Rubber.

These comfortable and simple chairs were originally designed for the tired executive, who was no doubt expected to exchange them for some million-dollar backbreaker when he or she sat down to dine. Why not eat in comfort as well?

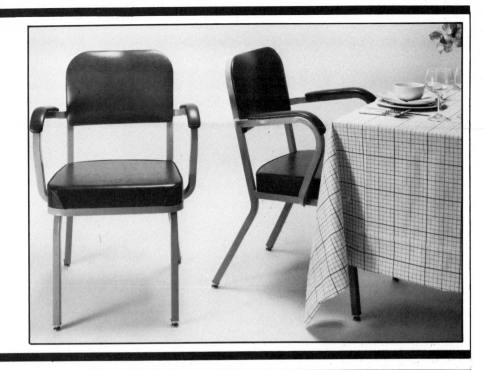

Conference Side Armchairs: Steel frame, foam seat, Naugahyde fabric in black, brown or green, $57.55. Crown Discount.

Place mats really are a sensible alternative to tablecloths, and the days when they were only permissible for breakfast at the kitchen table have passed. If you still can't quite bring yourself to use them for "real" dining, this wire glass may help convince you: there's absolutely nothing sloppy about it.

Wire Glass Place Mats: Polished baroque wire netting, about $15.00. Mfg'd by C-E Glass, available from Central Glass (and local glass suppliers).

Steel Folding Chairs: (left) *Steel frame, baked enamel finish in gray, beige, brown, blue or green. Upholstered in tan, blue, brown, green, gray, black or gold, $12.19.* (right) *Plain, $8.48. Both sold in multiples of five. C&H Distributors.*

These basic steel folding chairs have to be one of the last great buys around. When not in use they can be stashed in a closet or even hung on a wall. They also come with upholstered seats and backs, and can be found in many housewares and department stores in bright colors, but be wary: the real thing may be shoulder to shoulder with a poor imitation, so take a good look before you buy from a store.

Director's Chair: Metal frame, canvas seat, red, brown or white, $37.00. Conran's.

A variation on the more familiar wood frame director's chair. These have a light tubular metal frame and an open, unfussy look. And like the other director's chair, they fold flat.

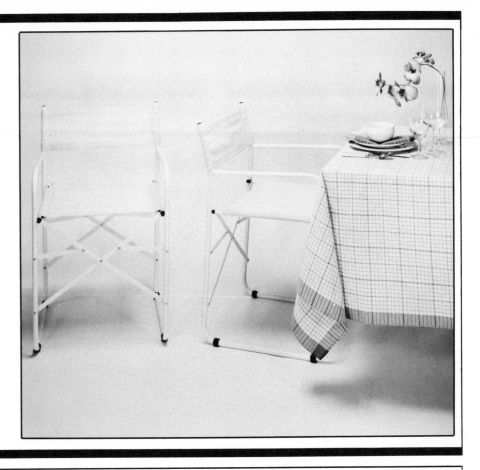

Bentwood Chair: Hardwood frame, walnut finish, vinyl upholstered seat in black, gold, persimmon or red, $75.00. American Hotel Register.

The familiar Bentwood restaurant chair. You're not going to buy a dozen of these to keep in the garage for spare seating—they're not cheap—but neither are they cheaply made. They have a pleasingly delicate look, but this version (cheaper, flimsier copies exist) is a very sturdy chair.

107

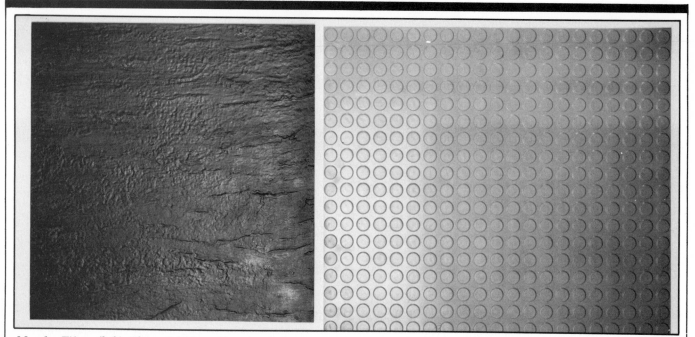

Mondo Tiles: (left) Slate #218, rubber in dark gray or burgundy, $3.90 per square foot. (right) Style MT, rubber in black, $2.35 per square foot; in terra cotta, beige, dark or light gray, blue, green or brown, $2.65 per square foot. All from Allstate Rubber.

EZ Sweep: Vinyl in black, brown, green or terra cotta, 24" wide rolls, $6.80 per linear yard, Pawling Rubber.

We're showing a selective sampling of rubber tiles and mats, none cheap but all lower-priced alternatives to the famous names of the field. All of them are quite easy to install, and we suggest you think of using them in small as well as large areas. You don't need to cover a kid's room or kitchen floor with them, but in a play area and around the work counter or sink they'll be particularly useful.

All of these tiles look great and wear like iron, and they're well worth using off the floor as well. Try them on table tops—but not for writing surfaces. You can also make an elegant tray by mounting tile on wood and attached drawer pulls for handles.

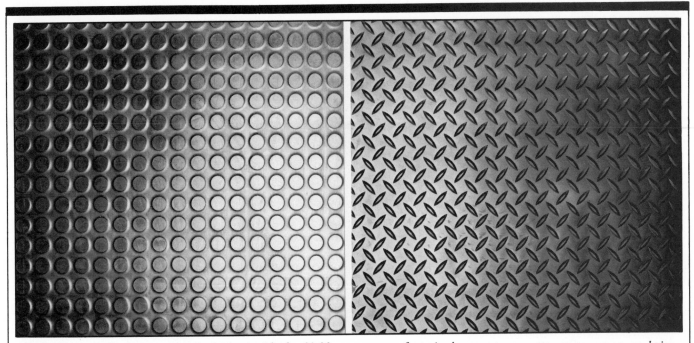

Global Tile: (left) Rubber, $^5/_{32}$" thick, in black, $3.22 per square foot; in brown, terra cotta, green, gray or beige, $3.78 per square foot. U.S. Mat & Rubber. *Dekplate:* (right) Vinyl, $^1/_8$" thick, 36" wide rolls, black or gray, $9.90 per linear yard. U.S. Mat & Rubber.

Mondo Tile: Style MC, rubber in terra cotta, beige, dark or light gray, blue, green or brown, $3.00 per square foot; in black, $2.65 per square foot. Allstate Rubber.

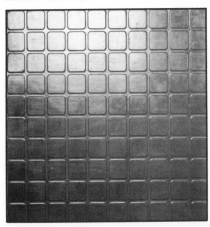

Table Bases: (left to right) Cast iron, matte black enamel, $49.50. L&B. Diagonal base, cast iron, 22", $25.25. L&B. Column diagonal, black or chrome (comes with Formica top). Mfg'd by Falcon, available from C&H Distributors. Table Top: Butcher block Formica, $69.87 (includes table base shown on right). Mfg'd by Falcon. C&H Distributors.

Restaurant table bases can be had from institutional suppliers for as little as $25.00. If you've ever shopped for this kind of table you know what an impressive figure that is. What's more, you don't need to run into great expense when fitting a top. While butcher block is beautiful but costly, your local lumber yard also carries cut plywood and pressboard. If you're planning on a paint finish, use the less expensive pressboard. Make the top at least 1 inch thick, and solve the problem of the unattractive edge by either sealing and painting the edge or attaching a thin strip of wood, such as lattice or molding, with thin finish nails.

In the photograph above we've matched an L&B table base with a C&H Distributors top to show that in this category components needn't be made for each other to look good together.

By the way, you should know that in the case of the table bases, you're dealing with what retailers would call a "second." You can get bases which are returnable if the finish is even slightly scuffed or scratched, but at *very* different prices. (We obviously don't think this a very serious drawback, but we thought you should understand that this line of product is different in this one respect.)

Most of those pans—unadorned with decals or cute flourishes—are supplied to cleaning professionals. You've probably seen the long-handled lobby pans before, and they're surrounded by plain old dustpans, which have it all over new, improved dustpans. They're cheap, and unlike most plastic pans, will last several lifetimes.

Dustpans et al.: (clockwise from top left) Janitor's steel, 12" edge, corrugated, black enamel, $2.24. American Hotel Register. Janitor's heavy, 12", reinforced hood, black, $3.75. American Hotel Register. Janitor's steel, black enamel, reinforced ribs, 12", $2.60. Beam Supply. Janitor's heavy duty, steel, 15", $4.43. American Hotel Register. Lobby pan, black, enamel finish, lacquered wood handle, $7.50. Beam Supply. Economy lobby pan, steel, nonclosing open front, double steel wire handle, 30", $8.62. American Hotel Register. **Brooms:** (left) Corn, red or black handle, $2.00; (right) Orchestra whisk, corn, $8.50. Both from Beam Supply.

It's relatively easy to think about the design of workplaces because their use is so specific and singular. An office at home doesn't usually have to perform one function during the day and another at night, and a sewing table needn't be practical at one moment and look elegant to your dinner guests the next.

The great barriers for most of us are expense and space. This chapter is devoted to showing you some of the ways you can sur-mount these obstacles with the aid of the right components. It should also help you get over the notion that the practical and the attractive are separate qualities. To give one example, there's no need to mount a battery of un-shaded lights over a workbench because "even if they're ugly, you need the light," when RLMs pro-vide as much illumination as you'll ever need *and* look good.

It's true that not everybody needs a work area, but if this book has encouraged you to think of your home as a space tailored to accommodate different activi-ties, you may already have re-alized that you spend significant amounts of time working at home. It could be only typing, fixing broken toys, keeping fam-ily accounts or repotting gerani-ums—but once you've got a space set up for that work you may wonder how you survived without it.

As far as expense is concerned, we can only really deal with the concept of value. We can't tell you how to set up an office for $21.95, but the items we show represent a minimal amount of money well spent. In fact we haven't always looked for the *cheapest* lamp or chair—though we hope we've at least pointed the way for people who must—but there isn't a table or light or storage component in this chapter that won't work well and wear well.

As for the second obstacle, space, we've shown a range of setups that require only a corner or an unused wall of a room. It's also our intention to introduce simple ideas and solutions to the problem of space that don't hinge on a particular object. Having come across the *idea* of a cart that can be rolled under the work table when not in use, you might decide to put your old two-drawer file cabinet on casters and use it in just that way.

To echo something said earlier, tasks sometimes become chores because the space you do them in is poorly planned. Whether it's reaching for pots on a shelf that's too high or typing while seated on a chair that's too low, the principle is the same: sometimes a hanging system or an adjustable drafting chair makes all the difference in the world.

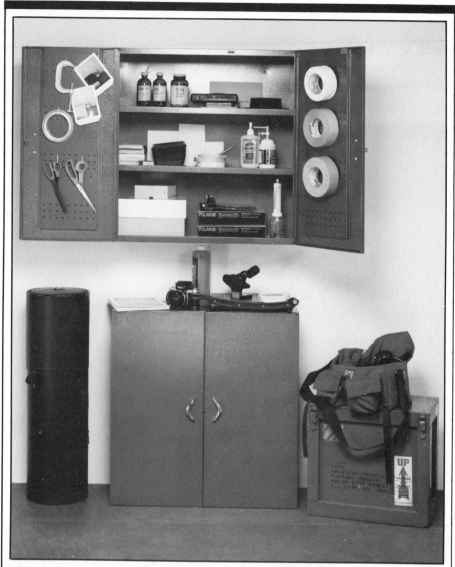

Wall Storage Cabinets: Steel, gray enamel finish, 30" h × 30"w × 12"d, steel pegboard doors, two shelves, $49.97. Mfg'd by Homak, available from C&H Distributors.

We just happened to have a photographer handy, so we equipped this steel cabinet for use in a photography studio. You've seen it in swanker settings, but in these shots it's back to absolute basics—wall-hung storage with hanging space on the insides of the doors. But don't let us discourage you from dressing it up and taking it out of the basement. The handles are easily replaced with more elegant ones, and the cabinet can be painted.

Sawhorses: Ladder-grade hardwood, rigid locking hinges, 30"d × 26"h, $26.22 per pair. Brookstone.

The beautiful and sturdy Brookstone sawhorses are shown with a top we strongly recommend. Particle board will set you back all of $13 to $15 for a 4-foot by 8-foot piece. That's the smallest sheet available, but at that price, you can use the unused portion for firewood. We suggest that you not use anything under a thickness of ¾ inch for a worktable.

Two routes to inexpensive worktables. The legs on the left may not be slender or delicate, but they're extremely strong and they can be bolted to a table top. And, if necessary, to the floor.

The sawhorses may not have the same kind of epic strength, but are very sturdy and beautiful.

Table Legs: (left) Steel, gray finish, 30"d × 32"h, $13.55 each. Mfg'd by Edsal, available from C&H Distributors. (Also available in 36"d × 32"h.) Sawhorses: (right) Rigid locking hinges, ladder-grade hardwood, 30"d × 26"h, $26.22 per pair. Brookstone.

Two solid chairs that will be with us when the transparent plastic Italian Award winner (It's a chair! It's a goldfish tank!) is just a faded memory. On the left is a drafting chair with a footring, which is available with vinyl upholstery and can be fitted with casters. The chair on the right not only has a somewhat imposing name—secretarial posture chair—but has about the best movements of any rolling chair we've seen.

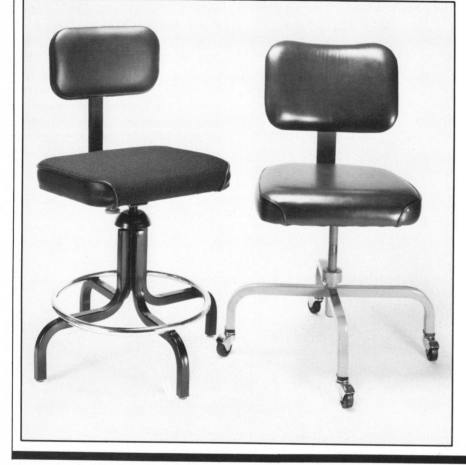

Drafting Chair: (left) Steel frame in black, silver, gray, green and other colors; vinyl back and vinyl or fabric seat in blue, brown, black, red, gray or avocado; height adjusts 21–26", $63.65. Mfg'd by Eck-Adams, available from C&H Distributors. (Also available in 26–31" height and with casters.) *Secretarial Posture Chair:* (right) Steel frame, Naugahyde upholstery in green, black or brown; adjustable back angle, height, back height; on casters, $62.89. Crown Discount.

Same bins, different panel. This bench rack simply moves the system off the wall and onto a table or counter top. With the rack, needless to say, you can also move the whole thing easily. When ordering, remember that you can either purchase the rack separately or in combination with bins.

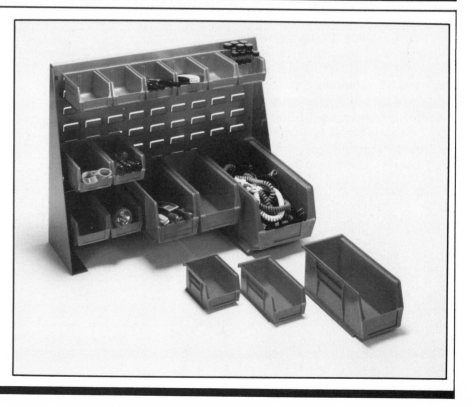

Bench Rack: Steel, enamel finish, gray 35 3/4"w × 19"h, $24.78. Mfg'd by Akro-Mils, available from C&H Distributors. *Akro-Bins:* Polypropylene (tough plastic) in red, blue or yellow. Smallest is 5 3/8" × 4 1/8" × 3", $.55. Largest is 10 7/8" × 5 1/2" × 5", $2.49. Mfg'd by Akro-Mils, available from C&H Distributors. (Some of the smaller bins are available only in 1-dozen lots.)

This picture is dedicated to all who feel they have to hold off on a sewing (or whatever) room until: a) the twins (now 4½) grow up and leave home; b) you build an extra wing on your apartment; c) a wealthy relative considerately dies and bequeaths you a castle on the Rhine; or d) all of the above.

All we've used is a drafting chair, a set of the smaller RLM dome lights and the common lunchroom folding table. The table provides a great deal of surface, the lights will give you excellent illumination (they take bulbs up to 200 watts) and the chair is, after all, designed for working. In all, a workplace that doesn't require vasts amounts of money or effort, or even a permanent installation.

Folding Table: Steel legs, top in beige masonite or plastic laminate (tan, birch, walnut or teak finish), 72"l × 30"d × 29"h, $47.24. Mfg'd by Correll, available from C&H Distributors. (Also with adjustable-height legs). **Drafting Chair:** *Steel frame in black, silver, gray, green and vinyl back and vinyl or fabric seat in blue, black, brown, red, gray or avocado, height adjusts 21–26", $63.65. Mfg'd by Eck-Adams, available from C&H Distributors. (Also available in 26–31" height and with casters.)* **Small Dome RLMs:** *Porcelain enamel (10" diameter) in white, red, green, blue, yellow and black, up to 200 watts, $35.00. Abolite.*

A small but self-contained work area that should last for generations. The rolling cabinet and workbench are both steel and both as solid as a rock. The cabinet and adjustable stool can even be housed under the table if your work area is sharing a space also used for other purposes.

The letter tray is a snappy little number from the Elfa system, and it can hold up to three trays which swivel on the stand. The clock is a little expensive, but it should also last well into the Digital Age. The aluminum-framed marker board is made of white porcelain. It takes both Dry-Erase felt markers (which, as the name implies, can be erased with a dry cloth) and permanent markers, which are easily wiped off by a wet cloth.

Workbench: Steel, baked enamel finish in red or gray, 48"l × 29"d × 34"h, $99.65. Shure Mfg. (Available in other sizes, with industrial butcher block tops, casters.) *Rolling Cabinet:* Steel, pegboard door, gray with red door, 22 1/2"w × 15"d × 29"h, 3" casters, two shelves, $47.81. Mfg'd by Homak, available from C&H Distributors. *Cambridge Adjustable Stool:* Hardwood, varnished seat, steel legs in black, brown, yellow, green or white baked enamel, $39.50. Charrette's. *Remarkable Marker Board:* Aluminum frame, white porcelain on steel surface, 36"w × 24"h, $55.00. Crown Discount. *Electric Clock:* 10" diameter, black, white or colored frame, $54.50. Peter Pepper Products. *Elfa Letter Tray #540:* White epoxy-coated wire, one stationary, two swivel baskets, white or brown, 15 1/2"l × 10 3/4"w, $30.00. Scan Plast. *Standard Dome RLM:* Porcelain-on-enamel in white, blue, green, yellow, black or red, 14" diameter, 150 watts, about $35.00. Abolite. (Available in other sizes.)

These have been around forever, and when an object survives for years with no basic design "improvements"—the Volkswagen Beetle comes to mind—you have to assume it was made right in the first place. The height adjustment is in the legs, which telescope to a low of 24 inches and go up to 33 inches.

Metal Stools: Steel frame, gray enamel finish, telescopic legs (height adjusts 24–33"). (left) Masonite seat, $30.27. (right) Gray vinyl-padded upholstered seat and back, $39.23. Both from C&H Distributors.

Luxo lights are classics in the best sense of the word—totally simple and totally functional. It's hard to imagine improving on their design or tiring of their looks. They can be used with different types of mount, and in one movement can be transformed from general (bounced off the wall or ceiling) to task (direct) light. What else is there to add, other than that they're well made and reasonably priced.

For a pleasant surprise, by the way, check out the price of that handsome fruit bowl.

Luxo Crownlights: Porcelain enamel shade in red, black, white, yellow, blue, orange, brown, green or gray, 36" arm, clamp-on or wall-mount component included, $19.50. Thunder and Light. Luxo Light Mounts: (left) Weighted base, $21.75. (center) Wall mount, $4.40. Available in red, black, white, yellow, blue, orange, brown, green, gray or chrome (slightly more). (right) T-Stand with casters, chrome pole, aluminum base, $66.95. Mfg'd by Luxo, available from Thunder and Light. Battery Jar: Laboratory glass, 1 gallon, $5.75. Arthur H. Thomas.

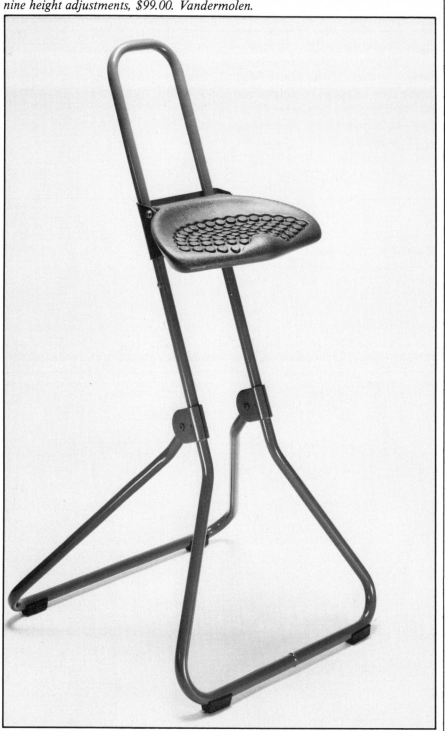

If you're putting a kitchen or workroom together on a shoe-string budget, you can probably live without these. They are made for laboratories, and are entirely of steel, much of it with a high-quality baked enamel finish.

There is, of course, the "if you buy good you get good" attitude. They're truly handsome and won't have to be replaced for years.

Laboratory Stools: Steel frame, perforated steel seat, adjustable height 16–30", baked enamel finish. (left) Without footring, $60.48. (right) With footring, $77.76. Arthur H. Thomas.

If we had used a computer to select items for this book, the machine would have cut this chair from the list. It's right at the $100 limit and it's only a chair, an armless one at that.

But this is an object no flesh-and-blood person can easily resist. Its bright red frame and black seat fold flat so it can be hung or easily stowed away for storage, and it has not two or three but *nine* seat positions, ranging from the level of a low seat to a top position where you're leaning back while almost fully upright. That helps explain why it's standard in many European factories, and one brief glance tells you why we couldn't bring ourselves to leave it out of this book.

120

Steel Worktable: Gray steel, 1" thick flakeboard top, 60"l × 30"d × 34"h, $62.27. Mfg'd by Edsal, C&H Distributors. Wall Storage Cabinet: Steel, baked enamel finish in gray, 30"h × 30"w × 12"d, steel pegboard doors, two shelves, $49.97. Mfg'd by Homak, available from C&H Distributors. Shop Chair: Steel, swivel, height adjusts 21–27", hardboard panel seat (15" square), $29.39. Charrette's. Casters (not shown) available, $8.00 additional. High-Impact Shop Trays: (under cabinet) Plastic, impact-resistant, in seven colors, $1.65 each. Keystone Optical. Photographer's Light: Steel stand in black, extends 3–8', aluminum boom arm (44" long), swivel socket, aluminum reflector (8" diameter) in red, yellow, green, blue, brown or white, up to 250 watts, $65.00. Smith Victor.

Here we've set up a work space for a non-living area, such as a studio. The two main components are the steel and flakeboard worktable and the cabinet suspended above it. Note the pegboard on the insides of the doors.

The super-flexible light is elegant enough for an entrance hall, but the steel work chair, with its hardboard seat, is a less sophisticated object—it truly belongs in this type of setting.

How to Paint Steel

Many of the metal items in this book come in standard gray, but there's no reason to pass up a good item simply because that's not the color you want. It can be painted, but you need to know how.

The first thing you need to do before painting is to break the surface of the finish by sanding with coarse sandpaper so as to allow the new paint to adhere properly.

Use air-drying enamel finishes and expect to paint two coats, sanding lightly again after the first coat. Light colors will sometimes require additional coats. Spraying is best for a smooth finish, but apply many light coats as heavy spraying will result in drips and runs. And be sure to follow the instructions on the spray can. Using a brush to paint is also possible but use a *good* brush and apply paint (especially the finish coat) smoothly and evenly, and in a consistent direction.

The same applies to unfinished steel but you should first remove the oily film on the steel with a naphtha-type solvent, readily available at most hardware stores. Be extremely careful with the flammable solvent and follow precautions to the letter.

But don't worry, there really aren't too many items in the book that will come to you unfinished. And, as we noted elsewhere, some manufacturers—Shure, Equipto, and Able included—offer factory finishes in various colors for an additional charge, saving you the trouble of painting.

There are some people who are perfectly happy using the kitchen table for a desk, as often as not the type who can sleep in armchairs. But they're in the minority, and this setup shows that the rest of us needn't go without an office at home for want of money or space.

Here a typing stand is used as a small desk and a newsstand rack makes a space-saving container for magazines, sketch pads or even files. The drafting chair is the single costliest item, but that's as it should be—a desk without a sturdy and comfortable chair is a desk in name only. In all, an attractive and practical arrangement that requires no great expense and can be set up in almost any unused corner of the home.

Typing Stand: Metal, sand, gray, black or walnut finish, locks on two front wheels, $52.00. Crown Discount. **Electric Clock:** *White dial, black numerals and hands, 12" diameter, $19.92. Mfg'd by P&I Ind., available from C&H Distributors. (Also available with 8¹/₂" diameter. Battery-operated available, slightly higher.)* **Newsstand Rack:** *Steel 9³/₄"w × 65" h, twenty-three pockets, 8¹/₂" deep, baked enamel finish in black, tan or gray, $49.37. Mfg'd by Durham Mfg., available from C&H Distributors.* **Drafting Chair:** *Steel frame in black, silver, gray, green and other colors, vinyl back and vinyl or fabric seat in blue, brown, black, red, gray or avocado; height adjusts 21–26", $63.65. Mfg'd by Eck-Adams, available from C&H Distributors. (Casters, and a 26–31" version are available.)*

Wall-Mounted Worktable: Steel, baked enamel in red or gray, 48"l × 29"d surface, $85.10. Shure Mfg. (Available in other widths and depths as well.) **Drafting Chair:** *Steel frame, baked enamel finish in black or gray, vinyl seat in black or green, height adjusts 20–26", $82.50. Charrette's.* **Louvered Panel:** *Steel, 19" high, slots for Akro-bins, $14.66. Mfg'd by Akro Mils, available from C&H Distributors.* **Akro-Bins:** *Polypropylene in red, blue or yellow, range of sizes between $.55 and $6.97 each. Mfg'd by Akro-Mils, available from C&H Distributors.* **Flexible Clamp-On Lamp:** *Enamel finish in black, swivel shade, 18" flexible arm, 75-watt bulbs, wall or desk mount, $16.88. Mfg'd by Prestige Products, available from C&H Distributors.* **Two-Drawer Tool Toter:** *Steel, baked enamel in gray, rubber casters, 32 1/2 "h × 14"w × 20"d, $73.77. C&H Distributors.*

Faced with a choice between lots of color reproductions and a reasonably priced book, we chose the latter. This picture brings home the painfulness of that choice, because—though gray and cold in black and white—the brightly colored plastic bins, the shiny black light and the fire engine red table and waste receptacle look spectacular in real life.

So try and imagine the plastic Akro-Bins in many colors. They're widely varied in size and shape and comprise, with their wall-mounted louvered panel, a defiantly straightforward open storage system. A close look at the steel worktable, wall mounted with feet resting on the ground, will help you see why it's tremendously sturdy. The lamps are fully flexible and surprisingly inexpensive.

"Go to your room!" is a phrase most of us remember from childhood, and as often as not we heard it when we were being punished. One obvious implication was that the kid's room was the last place any youngster wanted to actually spend time. What a strange idea.

Design for kids is clearly different than design for adults—for one thing, success is quite often unrelated to cost. After all, it's the box the $500 toy comes

Kids

in that's often more interesting to a child than the toy itself. But while there's no single approach to designing a kid's space, there are two things to keep in mind: children are smaller than adults, and they're much more energetic.

A good designer will also operate with the knowledge that children's rooms are different from the rest of the house in that they are *their* places for play, work or fooling around with friends—the only area in the house that's not adult turf. By the way, the fact that kids are smaller may not be as obvious a consideration as it first seems. To give one example, kids are less likely to put their toys away if their storage area is on the top shelf of a closet than if it's close to the ground.

Another "obvious" consideration: a child's room shouldn't be expected to stay the same. Let's face it, consistency of taste is a more or less adult charac-teristic. So *you* may elect to spend thousands on your French Provincial dining room, but an expensive "look" doesn't make sense for the kid's spaces.

Remember that the basic materials in the room are going to have to contend with mistreatment—you might hope that a seven-year-old will be respectful with your furniture, but now we're talking about the one room in which kids ought to be free to act like kids. The walls and the floor are going to bear the brunt of the rough treatment over the years—the somersaults, spills, ball bounces and indiscriminate use of crayons, watercolors and things you're better off not thinking about. Materials like rubber and vinyl tile, sisal matting and gym pads have been used by industry for years because they bear up under constant abuse. And blackboard or homasote bulletin boards will protect walls through generations of chalk and crayon artists.

As you'll see here, using these materials does not automatically impose an industrial look on the room. You have to work a lot harder, and spend much more money to create one of those cold, gimmicky rooms, usually designed by adults to impress other adults, which you've seen in magazines.

Here we're basically showing various forms of storage, all of which are space saving and appropriate for a younger person. The hammocks, made for use on boats, are an excellent compromise between the adult ideal of having things out of sight when not in use, and the desire to have toys, dolls, basketballs or whatever within easy reach. Some kids might want a large desk to spread their homework out on, but others will find this fold-up nurse's desk enormously pleasing. The drafting stool is a low 18 inches, and the light can be rotated or picked up and moved around quite easily.

Double-Tier Locker: Steel, baked enamel, red, gray, tan or green, 12"w × 12"d × 60" h, approximately $79.00 per unit (three shown). Mfg'd by Penco, available from C&H Distributors. Fold-Away Nurse's Desk: Steel surface, 16" × 20", back pocket sections, green, beige, white, walnut, $43.56. Mfg'd by Budget Buddy Company, available from C&H Distributors. Gear Hammock: Mesh net, 4' long, white or green, $6.25. Manhattan Marine. Wooden Drafting Stool: Birch, 18" high, $41.30. Charrette's. Photography Light Stand and Reflector: Black steel light stand, extends 3 1/2–6 1/2', aluminum reflector (5" diameter) in red, yellow, green, brown, blue, white (oyster), $33.00. Smith Victor.

Did someone say storage? Multitier lockers serve to contain shoes, toys, sweaters ... and all the weird objects which adolescent girls collect. Baskets made by Elfa for the office also adapt effortlessly to a teenager's needs. The basket hanging on the park chair, though, has nothing to do with either offices or bedrooms—it's a bike basket.

*Multitier Locker: Steel, baked enamel finish in red, green, tan or gray, each box 12"w × 12'h × 12"d, approximately $85.00 per five-tier section (three shown). Mfg'd by Penco, available from C&H Distributors. **Elfa Wire Baskets:** (left of lockers) Letter baskets 11 ³/₄" × 15 ¹/₂"h, $11.00. Waste paper basket, 17"w × 25 ³/₄"h, $16.00. (right of lockers) In and out trays, 12 ¹/₄"w × 21 ¹/₄"h, $19.00. (arm of chair) Bike baskets, $14.00. All available from Scan Plast. **Folding French Park Chair:** Steel frame, wood back and seat, white, $61.00. Conran's.*

You may find that if your teenager has a room adapted to his or her style you won't have to constantly nag them to tidy it up. In any case, that phrase often means "make it look more like an adult's room." If they're not living in a neatly compartmentalized way, why saddle them with a room divided into neat compartments? The locker room bench, the single-tier lockers and Elfa bike baskets all make for loose but manageable storage.

Single-Tier Locker: Metal, baked enamel finish in red, gray, green or tan, 12"w × 12"d × 60"h, coat hooks and hat shelf inside, ventilation louvers on doors, approximately $68.00 per unit (three shown). Mfg'd by Penco, available from C&H Distributors. **Chalkboard:** *Magnetic, 18" × 24", green slate on metal, attached chalk rail, $20.00. Crown Discount.* **Spring Clamp Light:** *Aluminum reflector (8" diameter) in bright red, yellow, green, blue, brown or oyster, up to 250 watts, about $21.00. Smith Victor.* **Bike Baskets:** *Epoxy-coated wire, white, $14.00. Mfg'd by Elfa, available from Scan Plast.* **Bench:** *Top: hardwood, 9½"w × 4'l, $41.62; pedestals: steel, 17½" high, each $14.57. C&H Distributors.*

Despite their important-sounding name, Educubes are basically lightweight plastic blocks shaped to form seats or tables. While educators may see more sophisticated potential in them, we show them as tough, colorful furniture for children. One clever feature which you may already have noticed is that each cube offers two seats: the cube at left shows the lower while the one in the center—the identical cube flipped over—has a higher seat. And turned over they're tables.

Educube: Polyethylene blocks, 15" cube, red, blue, yellow and green, $90.00 set of four. Learning Products.

We all owe a vote of thanks to those hardy types who get out there in the rain and shine to brave the bugs and the beasts of the great outdoors. For without campers a whole world of portable, strong and durable objects might never have come into being.

The chair on the left is available as a stool (i.e., without the back) and the same is true of the chair on the right, which can be ordered with or without either pouch or back. All are made of aluminum and all fold flat.

Woodsman Camping Chair: (left) Aluminum frame, canvas or denim seat, blue and assorted colors, 18" high, about $8.00. Tucker Duck and Rubber. (Also available without back.) Sportsman Series: Aluminum frame in olive drab, camouflage-patterned canvas seats and back. (center) Hunter's Chair with gear pouch, about $15.00. (right) Stool with over-the-shoulder carry strap, about $12.00. Tucker Duck and Rubber.

The Hallco shop desk was not built for the bargain basement—it's a solid piece of metal furniture which is priced accordingly. But it's a good height for school age kids, has a top which flips open and a storage compartment like a school desk. The stool we show here was chosen for its height—it's like many other models but adjusts from a low of 15 inches.

The stacking trays are optician's trays. They're brightly colored, impact-resistant and have slots for labels.

Hallco Shop Desk: Metal, baked enamel finish in gray, 36 1/2" × 24 1/2"d × 30"h, $88.00. Mfg'd by Hallowell, available from Lloyd Engineering. **Low-Height Locking Stool:** *Steel base, baked enamel finish in beige, gray, black or green, plywood seat and back, adjusts 15–21" high, $51.78. Mfg'd by Garrett Prod's, available from C&H Distributors.* **Optician's Trays:** *Impact-resistant plastic, seven colors, $1.65 each. Keystone Optical.* **Luxo Luminaire Light:** *24" arm, black, white, red, yellow or brown shade, $19.50. Thunder and Light.*

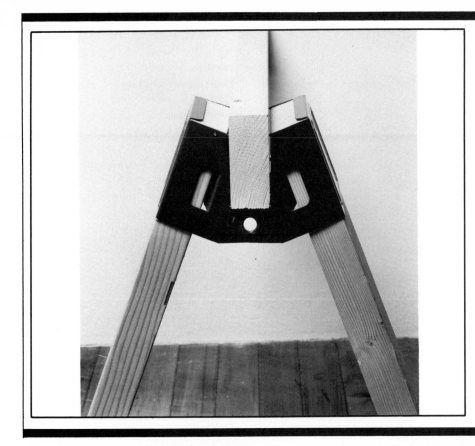

These sawhorse brackets are a sort of ultimate in design flexibility. With two pairs and a succession of inexpensive two-by-fours, you have a table which grows with your children: all you do is use progressively longer legs.

Sawhorse Brackets: Steel, blue finish, approximately $7.00 a pair. (Available at any hardware store.)

Canoe Chair: Aluminum frame, green canvas seat and back, 19¼"l × 14½"w × 5½"h, $16.00. L. L. Bean. Folding Stool: Steel legs in yellow, canvas seat in red or blue, 16½" high, $8.99. Mfg'd by Champion, available from I. Goldberg.

More small-fry furniture borrowed from campers and woodsmen. Lightweight, collapsible, easily handled by kids. If your youngsters are lucky enough to own their own yacht, they can take these with them on weekends. If not, they'll do fine in their room.

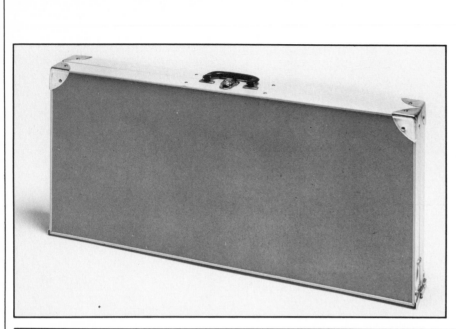

With the exception of those with the foresight to have chosen multimillionaire parents, most kids have to contend with some limitations on their space. This camping table, which folds and stores in a space only 4 inches wide, opens out to a generous surface almost 3 feet square. It also has a particularly pleasing design feature which makes it practical outdoors: it does not require a level surface to stand firmly.

And if you're old-fashioned enough to have large family get-togethers, it will come in handy as the kids' table.

Folding Camp Table: Steel top, baked enamel in black frame, yellow top and hardboard seats, $53.00. L. L. Bean.

There are times when the last thing in the world you need is a one-armed chair equipped with a surface for writing. But then there are other occasions when it's precisely what you need. This basic model folds away, as do the smaller, armless versions. The armless chairs are shown in various sizes. They're all cheap and, let's face it, cute as can be. The magnetic chalk-board speaks for itself, but it's worth pointing out that it costs no more than smaller, poorer-quality "message boards."

Children's Folding Chairs: Steel, baked enamel finish in beige, metallic blue, gray, green or tan. (left) Krueger Juvenile Chair, 12 1/2 " high seat, $12.59 (discounts on four or more). (center) Krueger Junior Chair, 15 1/2 " high seat, $13.17. Both available with upholstered seats from American Hotel Register. (right) Krueger Chair, steel frame and seat, baked enamel finish in beige, $7.99 (sold in multiples of five). C&H Distributors. **Tablet Armchair:** *(far right) Steel frame, baked enamel finish, plywood tablet desk, $33.30. American Hotel Register.* **Chalkboard:** *Green slate on metal, magnetic, aluminum frame, attached chalk rail, 18" × 24", $20.00. Crown Discount.*

Elsewhere we've sung the praises of hammocks as wall-hung storage. Now we're ready for the big leap into a whole new concept—actually sleeping in them! Sure, it's a crazy idea, but look at it this way—if it's comfortable for toys and dolls, why not for humans as well?

But in all seriousness, here are a few tips about using the larger hammock for your children and their overnight guests. Hang it low and anchor it firmly; that way they'll be able to act like kids in it without causing bodily harm to themselves and mental anguish to you, and it may not be a bad idea to have a mat or carpet underneath it. The large hammock can of course be put away when not in use—it folds to pocket size.

*Hammock: Nylon, 7'l × 20"w, $7.95. Mfg'd by Champion, available from I. Goldberg. **Gear Hammock:** Mesh netting, white or green, 4' long, $6.25. Manhattan Marine. **So Big Ruler:** Bright yellow, black letters, 6' high, meters and feet, $5.95. Childcraft.*

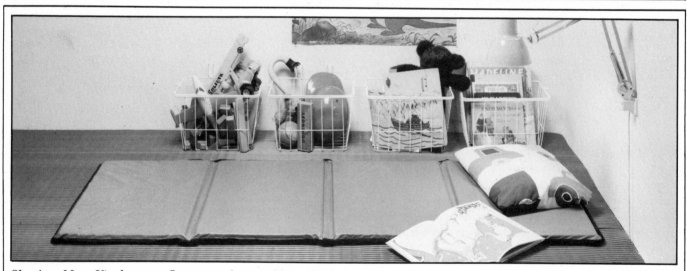

*Sleeping Mat: Vinyl cover, flame-retardant padding, 70"l × 25"w × 1"d, $13.95. Childcraft. **Bike Baskets:** Epoxy-coated wire, white, $14.00. Mfg'd by Elfa, available from Scan Plast. **Luminaire Luxo Lamp:** 24" arm, black, white, red, yellow or brown shades, $19.50. Thunder and Light.*

Childcraft's mat is comfortable to lie on and made of flame-retardant padding, which is never a bad idea. It also folds, which makes it especially convenient as a temporary guest bed or exercise mat.

The Luxo Luminaire lamp can also be moved—it lifts out of the wall-mounted socket to go elsewhere or even into a closet when it's not needed. The Elfa bike baskets make excellent, and equally portable, hold-alls for kids.

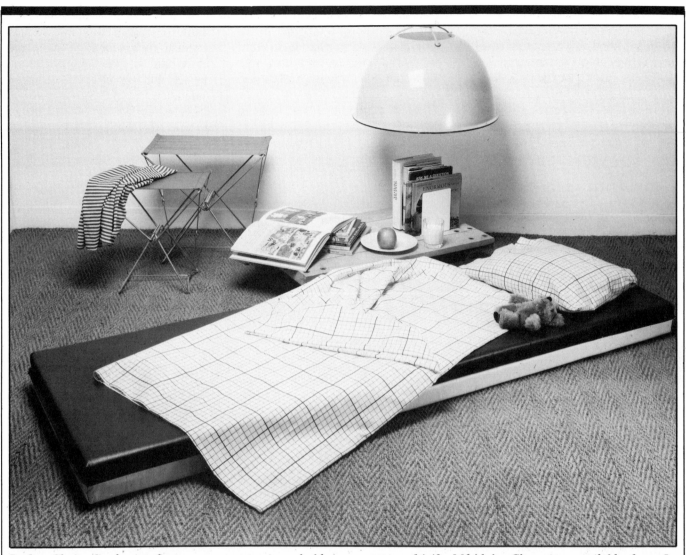

Pocket Chair: Steel wire frame, canvas seat in red, blue, or pattern, $4.49. Mfg'd by Champion, available from I. Goldberg. **Home Exercise Mat:** *Vinyl-coated nylon, two-color combinations of blue, red, yellow, green, white or gray, 2" thick urethane filler, $85.00. Jayfro Corporation.* **Deep Dome RLM:** *Porcelain enamel in yellow, green, brown, red, black or white, uplight, 20" diameter, $45.00. Abolite.* **Rolling Wood Pallet:** *Wood, 18" × 30", wheels, $38.80. A. Liss. (Other sizes available.)*

Any corner of the kid's room can be turned into a rest, snack or overnight guest area with the right equipment. All of these items (the light aside) are mobile and lightweight. The chairs, for instance, are hunters' stools originally designed to be carried in the woods. They fold down to practically nothing. The wood pallet is easily transported and stacked, and the bed here is a Jayfro tumbling mat which opens out to function as a safe surface for gymnastics. A word of warning: some take to sleeping on this kind of bed (foam on a hard surface) immediately; others need a few tries to get used to it. But almost all who do, find a regular bed uncomfortably soft thereafter.

This is basically just a piece of convoluted foam, ground sheet and straps, and there's no reason why you can't order the foam straight from one of the foam suppliers listed in your local Yellow Pages (in gray, light blue and white, usually about $3.00 per square foot). That's not to say it isn't comfortable to sleep on: it is, and it also happens to be perfect for use outdoors.

Trailmats Sleeping Pad: Polyurethane, lightweight, 75"l × 22"w × 2 1/2" thick, $12.99. Mfg'd by Champion, available from I. Goldberg.

If your kid is on the ball, he or she's going to want to know where the canoe is that goes with the canoe chair on the right. Sorry, but we just handle the design end.

The camp cot fortunately has nothing to do with canoes, but like the chair it's light and folds away. The roll-around boxes have obvious advantages over department store toy chests—they're kid height and can be rolled, inside the house and out.

WARNING: We've cheated with the light. It's a deep dome RLM—a classic industrial light which throws some light up as well as down, and you should suspend it by means of a hollow metal pipe (conduit). It's really too heavy to hang on its cord, as we've shown here.

The street sign can be custom ordered with any name. And if the kids want to know why other street signs don't also have their names on them, once again you're on your own.

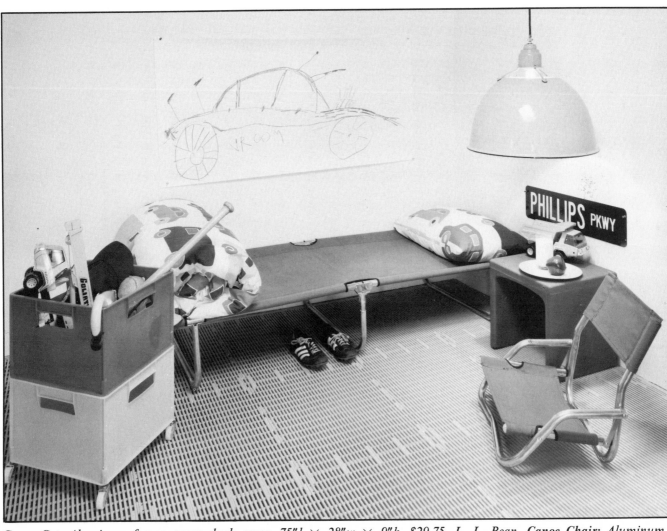

Camp Cot: Aluminum frame, green duck cover, 75"l × 28"w × 9"h, $29.75. L. L. Bean. Canoe Chair: Aluminum frame, green duck seat and back, folds, 19¼"l × 14½"w × 5½"h, $16.00. L. L. Bean. Roll-Around Boxes: Plastic, 14" × 14" × 10", red or yellow, casters, $29.95 for a set of two. Childcraft. Deep Dome RLM: Porcelain enamel, 20" diameter, red, white, yellow, blue, green or black, uplight, $53.00. Abolite. Please see warning below concerning how these lights should be suspended. Street Sign: White lettering, green baked enamel finish, $13.00. American Hotel Register. (Your choice of lettering.)

Access

Like all people who assemble this kind of list, we had a choice between creating the fattest-looking section possible or putting together a realistic section designed for people who are actually going to use it. We chose to do the latter, and have kept, with only a few exceptions, to sources we have had personal experience with.

As you read through the book and come upon specific items you'd like to purchase, or find out more about, you can turn to this section for ordering information under the manufacturer or distributor's name. Each listing consists of mailing address, phone number when applicable, shipping, catalog and payment information, and an indication as to which of these

sources will deal with you directly and which will refer you either to a local distributor or mail order source. Every company listed deals with the public in the way indicated, and almost none have stipulations we're aware of—such as buying in bulk quantities or minimum orders—that haven't been noted in the caption.

But it is important to realize that we're all on foreign soil here in the land of buying by the gross, bulk shipping and the like. Some

individuals will be patient and cooperative, others less so, but most will be unaccustomed to dealing with customers like yourself. With issues like buying single items, getting objects assembled that are normally sold unassembled and asking for a custom finish on a small item, you have to be both diplomatic and persuasive. Occasionally you can break a logjam by offering to pay a little more than list, but the important thing is that you realize that even a distributor who wants to sell to the public may find your request baffling. A little patience will go a long way.

Information about the availability, price and size of catalogs is also included, together with occasional comments. (You'll come to realize that these catalogs are as indispensable to this kind of merchandise as a card file is to a library.)

There are basically three types of sources listed: *distributors,* who will sell to you direct; *manufacturers,* who either sell to you direct or have listed distributors who do; and *retailers.* Even the largest manufacturer will be happy to refer you to a local supplier.

When we felt it would be useful for you to know about sources other than the ones we've personally dealt with, we've included them. We've asterisked them to remind you that *you* should ask about minimum quantities and types of acceptable payment and so on.

There are a number of other places where we suggest you continue your search. You should also take a look at the voluminous directory in Joan Kron and Suzanne Slesin's *High-Tech* (Clarkson N. Potter, 1978.

$29.95). It is a book of considerably different scope and intent, but in our opinion will long stand as the definitive work on the industrial aesthetic in home furnishings.

But the ultimate classic of the field is the Yellow Pages. Get to know what headings like "Materials Handling Equipment" and "Physicians & Surgeons' Equip. & Supls" mean and, when you're no longer easily intimidated, go to the nearest library and ask in your bravest voice for the Thomas Register, the twelve-volume guide to American manufacturers. There's an incredible variety of products out there, and every single one of them is listed.

Although we've gone to considerable trouble to find distrib-

the same legal protections when buying in this way that you have the rest of the time: the right to a warranty, adequate instructions, goods received in proper condition, return of unacceptable merchandise and so on.

This is also the place to say that although we are all in favor of improvising and experimenting, we've been careful not to endorse any potentially unsafe uses, and a manufacturer will do the same. It stands to reason that if a faulty light explodes when you switch it on, the manufacturer must accept the blame. Conversely, both manufacturers and authors must be protected from being charged with responsibility for accidents resulting from misuse of a product.

utors who will welcome retail customers, and have avoided listing those who were less than enthusiastic, we remind you that we *cannot guarantee* this information or even the merchandise. This is not a list of facts—it's a list of companies run by people who are not answerable to us. But they *are* answerable to the law, and we remind you that you have

Your best bet is to abide by the maker's directions, to let professionals handle anything you're not more than comfortable with and to use common sense and caution.

But don't let all this deter you from ever leaving your home again. It's one of those things that everybody knows already but needs to be said anyway.

ABC Foam Rubber Center
77 Allen Street
New York, NY 10002
(212) 431-9485

Retailer. Sells direct.
Catalog: Not available.
Payment: Check, COD, Visa.
Ships: UPS, parcel post.

Foam rubber of all types.

Able Steel Equipment Company, Inc.
50-02 23rd Street
Long Island City, NY 11101
(212) 361-9240

Distributor. Sells direct.
Catalog: 32 pp., no charge.
Payment: Check, COD.
Ships: Common carrier.

Distributors of steel shelving with good prices and excellent finishes. Able will build to individual specifications, but only if a sketch is submitted along with the dimensions. Color is extra.

Abolite Lighting, Inc.
Center and Wood Streets
West Lafayette, OH 43845
(614) 545-6381

Manufacturer. Sells through dealers.
Catalog: Information sheets available, no charge.

Major manufacturer of commercial and industrial lighting fixtures (including RLMs).

Distributors: Available from most commercial electrical distributors. Locate local outlets in the Yellow Pages.

Accessory Specialties
441 Saw Mill River Road
Yonkers, NY 10701
(914) 476-9000

Manufacturer. Sells through dealers.
Catalog: 44 pp., no charge.
Manufacturer of washroom and hospital accessories.

Distributors: (Partial list. Contact Accessory directly for others.)

Leroy Mashburn and Associates
PO Box 11037
512 Scholtz Road
Charlotte, NC 28210
(704) 523-7376

Robert Perry Associates
509 Lunt Avenue
Schaumburg, IL 60193
(312) 894-1700

W.H. Steele
2622 North Main Street
Los Angeles, CA 90031
(213) 223-3831

The Advance Products Company
1101 East Central
Box 2178
Wichita, KS 67201
(316) 263-4231

Manufacturer. Sells through dealers.
Catalog: 20 pp., no charge.

Audio-visual carts and other products.

Distributors: Contact Advance directly for names of dealers in your area.

Ajusto Equipment Company
PO Box 348
Bowling Green, OH 43402
(419) 244-4983

Manufacturer. Sells direct.
Catalog: 16 pp., no charge.
Payment: Check, COD, Visa, MasterCard.
Ships: UPS, common carrier.

Laboratory stools and chairs.

Algoma Net Company
1525 Mueller Street
Algoma, WI 54201
(414) 487-5577

Manufacturer. Sells direct.
Catalog: 4 pp., $.50.
Payment: Check.
Ships: UPS.

Benches, hammocks and hammock stands.

Allstate Rubber Corporation
105-12 101st Avenue
Ozone Park, NY 11416
(212) 526-7890

Distributor. Sells direct.
Catalog: 4 pp., $1.00.
Payment: Certified check, COD.
Ships: UPS, common carrier.

Distributors of a wide range of rubber flooring: Pirelli, Mondo and others.

American Hotel Register Company
2775 Shermer Road
Northbrook, IL 60062
(312) 564-4000

Distributor. Sells direct.
Catalog: 967 pp., $5.00.
Payment: Check.
Ships: UPS, common carrier.

Distributors of an enormous range
of products for hotels and
institutions. The extensive catalog is
well worth the price.

Appleton Electric Company
1701 West Wellington Avenue
Chicago, IL 60657
(312) 975-6300

Manufacturer. Sells through dealers.
Catalog: 90 pp., no charge.

Manufacturer of industrial RLM
and vaportight lights, as well as
other commercial lighting.

Distributors: (Partial list. Contact
Appleton directly for others.)

Allphase Electric Supply
PO Box 5263
Highway 220
North Martinsville, VA 24112
(703) 647-3731

General Electric Supply Company
1160 Springfield Road
Union, NJ 07083
(201) 964-5858

Graybar Electric Company
Church Street
Albany, NY 12202
(518) 436-4761

Westinghouse Electric Supplies
141 North 11th Street
Philadelphia, PA 19107
(215) 238-4500

Arista Surgical Supply Company
67 Lexington Avenue
New York, NY 10010
(212) 679-3694

Retailer. Sells direct.
Catalog: 24 pp., $1.50.
Payment: Check, MasterCard
(minimum order, $50.00).
Ships: UPS

Retailer of medical and laboratory
equipment.

Beam Supply Inc.
712 Broadway
New York, NY 10003
(212) 475-5253

Retailer/distributor. Sells direct.
Catalog: 100 pp., $2.00.
Payment: Cash, check, COD.
Ships: UPS, common carrier.

Industrial cleaning and maintenance
products.

L.L. Bean, Inc.
Casco Street
Freeport, ME 04033
(207) 865-4761

Retailer/mail order house. Sells
direct.
Catalog: 128 pp., no charge.
Payment: Check, MasterCard, Visa,
American Express.
Ships: UPS, parcel post (included in
price).

The catalog is a legend in its own
time and the stock of outdoor gear
is unequaled. L.L. Bean never closes
and you can order by phone 24
hours a day.

**Benjamin Division - Thomas
Industries Inc.**
Route 70 South
Box 180
Sparta, TN 38583
(615) 738-2241

Manufacturer. Sells through dealers.
Catalog: 80 pp., $1.00.

Commercial and industrial lights
and equipment, including RLMs.

Distributors: Available from most
commercial electrical distributors.
Locate local outlets in the Yellow
Pages.

Brookstone Company
475 Vose Farm Road
Peterborough, NH 03458
(603) 924-7181

Retailer. Sells mail order, direct.
Catalog: 68 pp., no charge.
Payment: Check, MasterCard, Visa,
American Express.
Ships: UPS, parcel post.

The hardware lover's L.L. Bean,
where housewares, cooking
equipment and hard-to-find tools
are specialties.

John Byron Displays Ltd.
220 West Park Avenue
Long Beach, NY 11561
(516) 431-0669

Distributor. Sells direct.
Catalog: 60 pp., $4.00.
Payment: Check.
Ships: UPS (FOB Hialeah, Florida).

Slat walls and accessories.

C&H Distributors, Inc.
400 South 5th Street
Milwaukee, WI 53204
(800) 558-9966

Distributor. Sells direct.
Catalog: 254 pp., no charge.
Payment: Check, COD,
MasterCard, Visa.
Ships: UPS, common carrier.

Mail order distributors who carry a
truly enormous range of items, from
safety equipment to shop tools,
materials handling supplies to
storage systems. Their prices and

catalog are excellent, and so is their
attitude—they are extremely
helpful.

**C-E Glass, Combustion
Engineering, Inc.**
825 Hylton Road
Pennsauken, NJ 08110
(609) 662-0400

Manufacturer.
Catalog: 16 pp., $1.00.

Manufacturer of safety glass,
insulating glass, automotive, pattern
wire, and plate glass.

Distributors: Partial list. Locate
local outlets in Yellow Pages under
Glass Dealers.
  Capitol Glass and Sash Co. Inc.
  550 Hudson Street
  New York, NY 10014
  (212) 243-4528

Cayne Equipment
93 Mercer Street
New York, NY 10012
(212) 226-1300; (201) 656-6789;
(516) 242-0190; (914) 997-0227

Manufacturer/distributor. Sells
direct.
Catalog: Information sheets.
available, no charge.
Payment: Check, COD.
Ships: UPS, common carrier

Steel shelving, lockers and lifting,
storage and handling equipment.

Central Dental Supply Company
168 North Franklin Street
Hempstead, NY 11550
(516) 483-6000

Distributor. Sells direct.
Catalog: Not available.
Payment: Check.
Ships: UPS.

Dental supplies and Good-Lite
lights.

Charrette Corporation
31 Olympia Avenue
Woburn, MA 01801
(212) 935-6000

Retailer. Sells direct.
Catalog: 272 pp., $2.00.
Payment: Cash, check, COD, Visa,
MasterCard, American Express.
Ships: UPS, common carrier.
Retailer of a full range of fine art
products, including drafting stools
and tables.

Childcraft Education Corporation
20 Kilmer Road
Edison, NJ 08817
(201) 572-6100; (800) 631-5262

Retailer. Sells direct.
Catalog: Growing Years Catalog, 185 pp., $1.50.
Payment: Cash, check, MasterCard, Visa, American Express.
Ships: UPS, common carrier (invoiced later).

Educational toys and materials for preschoolers to grade 3.

Conran's Mail Order
145 Huguenot Street
New Rochelle, NY 10801
(914) 632-0515

Main office:
160 East 54th Street
New York, NY 10022
(212) 371-2225

Retailer. Sells direct.
Catalog: 112 pp., $2.50.
Payment: Cash, check, MasterCard, Visa, American Express, Conran's credit card.
Ships: UPS, common carrier.

Conran's really does stock everything for the home, from sofas to dish towels. They pride themselves on the design—mostly clean and contemporary—of their merchandise. The catalog is an interior design course in book form.

Crown Discount Corporation
31-28 Queens Boulevard
Long Island City, NY 11101
(212) 37-7171; (516) 352-8844

Retailer. Sells direct.
Catalog: 600 pp., no charge.
Payment: Cash, check, COD, Visa, American Express.
Ships: UPS, company-owned truck (locally).

A huge catalog of office furniture and institutional supplies.

Daroma Restaurant Equipment Corporation
196 Bowery
New York, NY 10012
(212) 226-6774

Distributor. Sells direct.
Catalog: None available.
Payment: Cash, check.
Ships: UPS, common carrier, parcel post.

Restaurant suppliers with a full line of kitchen appliances and utensils at excellent prices.

Sid Diamond Display Corporation
379 Fifth Avenue
New York, NY 10016
(212) 889-3850

Manufacturer. Sells direct.
Catalog: Information sheets available, no charge.
Payment: Check.
Ships: UPS.

Display systems for commercial and residential use.

Early Winters Ltd.
110 Prefontaine Place, South
Seattle, WA 98104
(206) 622-5203

Retailer. Sells direct, mail order.
Catalog: 80 pp., no charge.
Payment: Cash, check, American Express, MasterCard, Visa.
Ships: UPS, parcel post.

Camping equipment. A terrific catalog.

Edmund Scientific Company
7082 Edscorp Building
Barrington, NJ 08007
(609) 547-3488

Distributor. Sells direct through mail order.
Catalog: 112 pp., no charge.
Payment: Check, American Express, MasterCard, Visa.
Ships: UPS (charges added to total order).
4,000 science-related products. The catalog is a lot more fun than you might have expected.

Equipto
225 South Highland Avenue
Aurora, IL 60507
(312) 859-1000

Manufacturer. Sells direct.
Catalog: 116 pp., $3.00.
Payment: Check.
Ships: Common carrier.

Consistently high quality steel
shelving, cabinets, and slotted angle
systems, as well as carts, tables and
workbenches. Units are shipped
from local distributors, and
excellent color finishes can be
ordered from the factory.

Some Equipto products for the
home are available at retailers. For
stores in your area, contact:

Raymor/Moreddi Inc.
734 Grand Avenue
Ridgefield, NJ 07657
(201) 941-0220

Max Finkelstein Inc.
28–40 31st Street
Long Island City, NY 11102
(212) 274-8900

Distributor. Sells direct.
Catalog: 30 pp., no charge.
Payment: Check, COD,
MasterCard, Visa.
Ships: UPS, common carrier, parcel
post.

Van and truck wheels for table
bases.

Goldberg's
902 Chestnut Street
Philadelphia, PA 19107
(215) 922-3436

Retailer. Sells direct, mail order.
Catalog: 83 pp., no charge.
Payment: Cash, check, MasterCard,
Visa, American Express.
Ships: UPS, common carrier.

Army-navy surplus, camping and
sports goods. $10.00 minimum
order by mail.

**Hallowell Division of S.P.S.
Technologies**
Township Line Road
Hatfield, PA 19940
(201) 337-1724

Manufacturer. Sells through dealers.
Catalog: 15 pp., no charge.

Industrial furniture: workbenches,
steel shelving, cabinets and carts.

Distributors: (Partial list. Contact
Hallowell directly for others.)

Lloyd Engineering Company
75 Rutgers Street
Belleville, NJ 07109
(201) 759-1900

Huffy Automotive Products
PO Box 1204
Dayton, OH 45401
(513) 866-6251

Manufacturer. Sells direct.
Catalog: 20 pp., $2.00.
Payment: Check.
Ships: UPS, common carrier, parcel
post (included in price).

A wide range of automotive service
equipment.

Import Specialists Inc.
82 Wall Street
New York, NY 10005
(212) 248-1633

Wholesaler. Sells only through
specialty and department stores.
Catalog: Information sheets
available, no charge.

Extensive selection of natural fiber
rugs, mats and runners, as well as
coco matting and the like.

Distributors: Contact Import
Specialists for the name of your
local retailer.

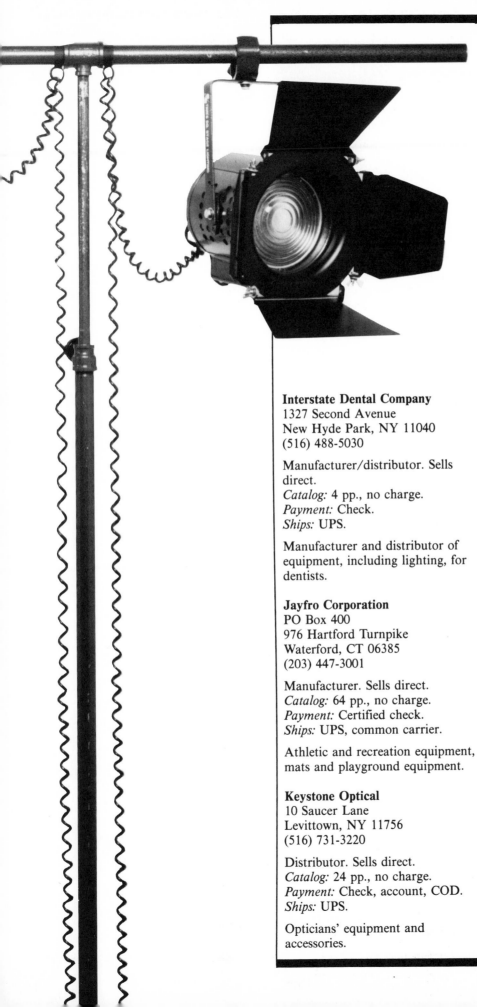

L&B Products Corporation
3232 Lurting Avenue
Bronx, NY 10469
(212) 882-5400

Manufacturer. Sells through dealers.
Catalog: Information sheets
available, no charge.

Restaurant table bases.

Distributors: (Partial list. Contact
L&B directly for others.)

Outwater Hardware Company
365 River Drive
Garfield, NJ 07026
(201) 772-7760

Learning Products, Inc.
10845 Baur Boulevard
St. Louis, MO 63132
(314) 997-6400

Manufacturer. Sells through school
distributors.
Catalog: 8 pp., no charge.

Manufacturer of preschool and early
learning materials.

Distributors:

Beckley-Cardy Company
1900 North Narragansett
Chicago, IL 60639
(312) 622-5420

Constructive Playthings
2008 103rd Terrace
Leawood, KS 66206
(913) 642-8244

J.L. Hammett Company
100 Hammett Place
Braintree, MA 02184
(617) 848-1000

Lakeshore Curriculum Materials
2695 East Dominguez Street
Carson, CA 90749
(213) 537-8600

Interstate Dental Company
1327 Second Avenue
New Hyde Park, NY 11040
(516) 488-5030

Manufacturer/distributor. Sells
direct.
Catalog: 4 pp., no charge.
Payment: Check.
Ships: UPS.

Manufacturer and distributor of
equipment, including lighting, for
dentists.

Jayfro Corporation
PO Box 400
976 Hartford Turnpike
Waterford, CT 06385
(203) 447-3001

Manufacturer. Sells direct.
Catalog: 64 pp., no charge.
Payment: Certified check.
Ships: UPS, common carrier.

Athletic and recreation equipment,
mats and playground equipment.

Keystone Optical
10 Saucer Lane
Levittown, NY 11756
(516) 731-3220

Distributor. Sells direct.
Catalog: 24 pp., no charge.
Payment: Check, account, COD.
Ships: UPS.

Opticians' equipment and
accessories.

A. Liss & Company
35-03 Bradley Avenue
Long Island City, NY 11101
(212) 392-8484; (800) 221-0938

Distributor. Sells direct.
Catalog: 170 pp., $1.00.
Payment: Check.
Ships: UPS, common carrier.

Distributor of many makes of
storage and materials handling
equipment: shelving, slotted angle,
casters and wheels bins, mirrors,
desks, chairs, containers.

Manairco Inc.
PO Box 111
Mansfield, OH 44901
(419) 524-2121

Manufacturer. Sells direct.
Catalog: Information sheets
available, no charge.
Payment: Check, COD.
Ships: UPS, common carrier, parcel
post.

Airport lighting equipment.

**Manhattan Marine and Electric
Company, Inc.**
116 Chambers Street
New York, NY 10007
(212) 267-8756

Retailer. Sells direct.
Catalog: 424 pp., $2.00.
Payment: Cash, check, American
Express, MasterCard, Visa.
Ships: UPS, common carrier.

Full range of marine equipment and
accessories.

The Charles Parker Company
290 Pratt Street
Meriden, CT 06450
(203) 235-6365

Manufacturer. Sells through dealers.
Catalog: 48 pp., $1.00.

Manufacturer of bathroom
accessories and equipment, grab
bars, etc.

Distributors: (Partial list. Contact
Charles Parker directly for names of
others.)

Building Products Inc.
3947 Excelsior Boulevard
Minneapolis, MN 55416
(612) 925-4944

Dixon Clubbuck and Associates
Inc.
11815 East Slousan Avenue
Santa Fe Springs, CA 90670
(213) 723-9851

JCF Sales
299 Madison Avenue
New York, NY 10017
(212) 697-7566

Specification Sales Inc.
3814 Marquis Drive, Suite 107
Garland, TX 75042
(214) 494-1551

Pawling Rubber Corporation
157 Maple Boulevard
Pawling, NY 12564
(914) 855-1000

Manufacturer. Sells through dealers.
Catalog: 29 pp., $.50.
Payment: Varies with distributor.

Wide range of mats and matting
products for residential, industrial
and commercial uses.

Distributors: Contact Pawling
directly for names of dealers in your
area.

Penco Products Inc.
Brower Avenue
Oaks, PA 19456
(215) 666-0500

Manufacturer. Sells through dealers.
(Contact Penco for the names of
dealers in your area.)
Catalog: 60 pp., no charge.

Lockers, shelving, storage racks,
benches, shop furniture and
worktables.

J.C. Penney Company, Inc.
1301 Avenue of the Americas
New York, NY 10019
(800) 257-7101

Retailer. Stores throughout the
country.
Catalog: 1,200 pp., no charge.

Automotive and outdoor equipment
featured in this book.

Peter Pepper Products
17929 South Susana Road
Compton, CA 90221
(213) 979-0815

Manufacturer. Sells through dealers.
Catalog: Brochure available, no
charge.
Ships: UPS, parcel post.

Architectural accessories: medical
chart holders, clocks, sand urns, etc.

Distributors: Contact Peter Pepper
Products directly for names of
dealers in your area.

Professional Kitchen
18 Cooper Square
New York, NY 10003
(212) 254-9000

Distributor/retailer. Sells direct.
Catalog: Not available.
Payment: Check, MasterCard, Visa.
Ships: UPS.

Professional quality cookware and
equipment at good prices.

Rennert Manufacturing Co. Inc.
93 Green Street
New York, NY 10012
(212) 925-1463

Manufacturer. Sells direct.
Catalog: Information sheets only, no
charge.
Payment: Check, COD.
Ships: UPS.

Manufacturer of a complete line of
moving equipment, including
quilted moving pads.

Result Manufacturing
712 Stewart Avenue
Garden City, NY 11530
(212) 222-0616

Manufacturer. Sells direct.
Catalog: 4 pp., no charge.
Payment: Check.
Ships: UPS, common carrier.

Plastic storage boxes and racks.

Scan Plast Industries Inc.
54 East 54th Street
New York, NY 10022
(212) 755-0423

Distributor. Sells direct.
Catalog: 8 pp., $.35.
Payment: Check.
Ships: UPS, common carrier.

Importer of Elfa wire baskets.

Scientific Products
1230 Waukegan Road
McGaw Park, IL 60085
(312) 689-8410

Distributor.
Catalog: Information sheets
available, no charge.
Payment: Certified check.
Ships: UPS, common carrier.

Distributes lab glass direct only on
items featured in this book.
Otherwise, $250 minimum order.
Will refer you to your local dealers
of same products.

Sears Roebuck and Company
Sears Tower
Chicago, IL 60684
(312) 875-8306

Retailer. Stores throughout the
country.
Catalog: Sears' Farm Catalog.
Payment: Cash, check, American
Express, MasterCard, Visa, Sears'
credit card.
Ships: Through own network.

Sears is so much a part of the
landscape that some people hardly
know it's there. Others have relied
on it for virtually all their retail
needs for generations. The farm
catalog alone is worth the price of
admission.

Shure Manufacturing Corporation
1601 South Hanley Road
St. Louis, MO 63144
(314) 781-2500

Manufacturer. Sells through dealers.
Catalog: 20 pp., $1.00.

Industrial furniture and shelving systems with beautiful finishes.

Distributors: (Partial list. Contact Shure directly for names of others.)

Equipment Specialists
5254 Kearny Willa Way
San Diego, CA 92123
(714) 565-9022

Manhattan Ad Hoc Housewares
842 Lexington Avenue
New York, NY 10021
(212) 752-5488

Milonski Inc.
415 North Euclid Avenue
St. Louis, MO 63108
(314) 361-0058

Ross Oil Company
P.O. Box 1273, I.A.B.
Miami, FL 33148
(305) 885-4545

Smith Victor Corporation
301 North Colfax
Griffith, IN 46319
(219) 924-6136; (800) 348-9862

Manufacturer. Sells through dealers and photography retailers.
Catalog: 4 pp., no charge.
Payment: Check, COD.

Photographic lighting equipment adapted for home use. Full range of bright reflector colors, tripods, etc.

For local retailers contact:

Raymor/Moreddi
734 Grand Avenue
Ridgefield, NJ 07657
(201) 941-0220

Steele Canvas Basket Company, Inc.
199 Concord Turnpike
Cambridge, MA 02140
(617) 864-9337

Manufacturer. Sells direct.
Catalog: 24 pp., no charge.
Payment: Check.
Ships: Common carrier.

Canvas items including laundry baskets used in hospitals and institutions.

Steiner Industries
2265 West St. Paul
Chicago, IL 60647
(312) 252-0800

Manufacturer. Sells direct.
Catalog: 16 pp., $1.00.
Payment: Check, COD.
Ships: UPS.

Manufacturers of mobile screens and room dividers in a variety of materials.

Storage Concepts Group
892 Broad Street
Newark, NJ 07102
(201) 643-2645

Distributor. Sells direct.
Catalog: 4 pp., no charge.
Payment: Check.
Ships: UPS, common carrier (prepaid).

Schaeffer containers, panels and bench racks.

Sun Glo Corporation
PO Box 348
Chappaqua, NY 10514
(914) 238-5111

Manufacturer. Sells by mail.
Catalog: 14 pp., no charge.
Payment: Check.
Ships: UPS.

Unfinished wood stools, etc.

Arthur H. Thomas Company
Vine Street at Third
PO Box 779
Philadelphia, PA 19105
(215) 574-4500

Distributor. Sells direct, mail order.
Catalog: 4 pp., no charge.
Payment: Check, COD.
Ships: UPS, common carrier, parcel post.

One of the largest and most cooperative mail order distributors of lab glass.

Thunder and Light Incorporated
171 Bowery
New York, NY 10002
(212) 966-0757

Retailer. Sells direct.
Catalog: 40 pp., $.50 if mailed (otherwise, no charge).
Payment: Check, MasterCard, Visa.
Ships: UPS.

Retailer of a wide but selective range of contemporary lighting fixtures. Excellent prices on most items, including Luxo architect's lights. Extremely helpful.

Times Square Theatrical
318 West 47th Street
New York, NY 10036
(212) 245-4155

Distributor. Sells direct.
Catalog: 66 pp., no charge.
Payment: Check, COD.
Ships: UPS (collect), common carrier.

Theatrical special effect lighting and stage equipment. Reasonably priced.

Tucker Duck and Rubber Company
2701 Kelly Highway
PO Box 4167
Fort Smith, AK 72914
(501) 782-8662

Manufacturer. Sells through retailers only.

Distributors: K-Mart, Woolco and J.C. Penney. Contact Tucker Duck and Rubber for names of other retailers in your area.

U.S. Mat and Rubber Company, Inc.
PO Box 152
Brockton, MA 02403
(617) 587-2252; (800) 343-5955

Manufacturer. Sells through dealers.
Catalog: 48 pp., no charge.

Industrial and commercial mats and floor coverings.

Distributors: Contact U.S. Mat and Rubber directly for names of dealers in your area.

Vandermolen Corporation
119 Dorsa Avenue
Livingston, NJ 07039
(201) 992-8506

Importer. Sells direct, and through dealers.
Catalog: 1 p., no charge.
Payment: Check.
Ships: UPS.

Stand-aid seats.

Distributors: Contact Vandermolen directly for names of dealers in your area.

Other Dealers/Manufacturers

Aborn Rubber Company Inc.
20 Greene Street
New York, NY 10013

Rubber mats and products

Acme Stayput Pad Company
295 Fifth Avenue
New York, NY 10016

Furniture van pads and equipment

Adapto Steel Products
PO Box 1660
Hialeah, FL 33011

Steel storage equipment

Adirondack Direct
219 East 42nd Street
New York, NY 10017

Advance Manufacturing Company
Silver Star Road
Orlando, FL 32808

Lawn furniture and umbrellas

Alfax Manufacturing
431 Canal Street
New York, NY 10013

Business and institutional furniture

Allied Mat & Matting Inc.
476 Broome Street
New York, NY 10013

Coco matting, mats and runners

American Athletic Equipment
200 American Avenue
Jefferson, IA 50129

Manufacturers of athletic equipment

Ascot Steel Equipment Co. Inc.
45–35 39th Street
Long Island City, NY

Banner Mat & Products Company
17 Mercer Street
Cincinnati, OH 45210

Rubber, cocoa mats

Belson Manufacturing Company, Inc.
PO Box 207
North Aurora, IL 60542

Park and recreational equipment

A. N. Brabrook Incorporated
548 West 53rd Street
New York, NY 10019

Duck boards

Business and Institutional Furniture Co.
611 North Broadway
Milwaukee, WI 53202

Business and institutional furniture

Cooks Supply Corporation
151 Varick Street
New York, NY 10013

Restaurant suppliers

Creutzburg Incorporated
Box 7
Paradise, PA 17562

Farm supplies and equipment

Darby Dental Supply
100 Banks Avenue
Rockville Centre, NY 11570

Dental supplies and equipment

Defender Industries
PO Box 820
255 Main Street
New Rochelle, NY 10801

Marine supplies

Frank Eastern Company
625 Broadway
New York, NY 10012

Business and institutional equipment

Edward Don and Company
2500 South Harlem Avenue
North Riverside, IL 60546

Restaurant suppliers

Elkay Products Company, Inc.
35 Brown Avenue
Springfield, NJ 07081

Materials handling supplies and
equipment

**Empire Food Service Equipment
Corporation**
200 Lafayette Street
New York, NY 10012

Restaurant equipment

Fidelity Products Company
705 Pennsylvania Avenue South
Minneapolis, MN 55426

Materials handling and office
suppliers

Frey Scientific Company
905 Hickory Lane
Mansfield, OH 44905

Scientific equipment

Abraham Friedman
550 Broadway
New York, NY 10012

Army-navy goods

H. Friedman and Sons
16 Cooper Square
New York, NY 10002

Restaurant supplies

Don Gleason's Campers Supply Inc.
Pearl Street
Northampton, MA 01060

Army-navy surplus and sporting
goods

Goldberg Marine
202 Market Street
Philadelphia, PA 19106

Marine supplies

J. L. Hammett Company
100 Hammett Place
Braintree, MA 02184

Educational supplies

Fred Hill and Company
D and Luzerne Streets
Philadelphia, PA 19124

Materials handling and storage
equipment

Hughey and Phillips Company
3050 North California
Burbank, CA 91904

Airport lighting

Industrial Handling Company, Inc.
137 Meacham Avenue
Elmont, NY 11103

Materials handling and storage
equipment

Industrial Products Company
7445 North Oak Park Avenue
PO Box 48022
Chicago, IL 60648

Materials handling supplies

Industrial Safety and Security Co.
1390 Neubrecht Road
Lima, OH 45801

Koffler Sales Corp.
4501 Lincoln Avenue
Chicago, IL 60625

Mats

Lab Glass Inc.
11 West Boulevard
Vineland, NJ 08360

Laboratory glass and equipment

Liberty Mountain Sports
PO Box 306
Montrose, CA 91020

Sporting and camping supplies

Lyon Metal Products
1933 Montgomery Street
Aurora, IL 60507

Manufacturers of steel equipment

Manhattan Ad Hoc Housewares
842 Lexington Avenue
New York, NY 10021

Retailer of high tech housewares

Material Flow Inc.
835 North Wood Street
Chicago, IL 60622

Materials handling supplies

HG Maybeck Company, Inc.
134–16 Atlantic Avenue
Richmond Hill, NY 11419

Carts

**Metropolitan Wire Goods
Corporation**
24–16 Bridge Plaza South
Long Island City, NY 11101

Manufacturers of Metro Erecta and
Super Erecta

Modern Optical Supply
333 Washington Street
Boston, MA 02108

Montgomery Ward
150 North Broadway
Albany, NY 12201

Motion Performance Parts Inc.
598 Sunrise Highway
Baldwin, NY 11510

Automotive wheels—specialized

New Haven Moving Equipment
37 Washington
East Haven, CT 16512

Movers' pads and equipment

Olesen Company
1535 Ivar
Los Angeles, CA 90028

Theatrical lighting

Outwater Plastics Inc.
99–101 Oresident Street
Passaic, NJ 07055

Industrial plastics

Perko Inc.
16490 North West 13th Avenue
PO Box 64000-D
Miami, FL 33164

Marine supplies

Pittsburgh Corning Corporation
800 Presque Isle Drive
Pittsburgh, PA 15239

Glass blocks

Prima Education Products
Division of Hudson Photographic
Industries Inc.
Irvington-on-Hudson, NY 10533

Educational products, films, etc.

Reliance Equipment Company
PO Box 338
Linden, NJ 07036

Materials handling and storage
equipment

Republic Steel Ind.
1038 Belden Avenue NE
Canton, OH 44705

Lockers, shelving, steel products

SASO-Sargent-Sowell Inc.
1185 108th Street
Grand Prairie, TX 75050

Signs, safety, construction aids,
clothing, police equipment

Sailing Equipment Warehouse
PO Box 2575
Olympia, WA 98507

Marine supplies, mail order

Silverman's Dental Supplies
Apollo Road
Plymouth Meeting, PA 19462

Dental suppliers, but shop around
and compare prices

Standard Equipment
3175 Fulton Street
Brooklyn, NY 11208

Business and institutional supplies,
materials handling equipment

Standard Handling Devices Inc.
PO Box 13T
9 Sycamore Avenue
Meford, MA 02155

Materials handling suppliers

**Standard School Equipment
Company**
Silver City, NC 27344

School desks, chairs, etc.

**Tubular Specialties Manufacturing
Inc.**
13011 South Spring Street
Los Angeles, CA 90061

Grab bars, shower seats, bathroom
equipment

U.S. General Supply Corporation
100 General Place
Jericho, NY 11753

Mail order army-navy surplus goods

Uncle Dan's Surplus Store
Dept. MYP
2440 North Lincoln
Chicago, IL 60614

Surplus army-navy supplies

Warehouse Marine
PO Box 2575
Olympia, WA 98507

Marine supplies

J. C. Whitney and Company
1917 Archer Avenue
PO Box 8410
Chicago, IL 60680

Large mail order automotive
supplier

Wilcox International Inc.
564 West Randolph Street
Chicago, IL 60606

Hotel and institutional furnishing
and equipment

Accessories:
clocks, magazine racks, ashtrays,
etc.

American Hotel Register
Brookstone
C&H Distributors
Charrette
Conran's
Crown Discount
Interstate Dental
Keystone Optical
Peter Pepper Products
Scan Plast Industries

Bathroom accessories

Accessory Specialties
American Hotel Register
Beam Supply
Conran's
Interstate Dental
Manhattan Ad Hoc Housewares
Manhattan Marine & Electric
HG Maybeck
Charles Parker
Scan Plast Industries
Scientific Products
Arthur H. Thomas
Wilcox International

Cabinets

Able Steel Equipment
Adapto Steel Products
Alfax Mfg.
Ascot Steel Equipment
Business & Institutional Furniture
C&H Distributors
Cayne Equipment
Crown Discount
Equipto
Fidelity Products
Fred Hill & Co.
A. Liss & Co.
Penco Products
Standard Equipment
Wilcox International

Camping and sports equipment

American Athletic Equipment
L. L. Bean
Early Winters
Abraham Friedman
Don Gleason's Campers Supply
Goldberg Marine
I. Goldbergs
Liberty Mountain Sports
Tucker Duck & Rubber

Children's furniture

American Athletic Equipment
L. L. Bean
Childcraft Education
Conran's
Early Winters
J. L. Hammett
Jayfro
Learning Products
HG Maybeck
Prima Education Products
Standard School Equipment
Storage Concepts
Sun Glo
Tucker Duck & Rubber

Construction systems

C&H Distributors
Equipto
Hallowell
A. Liss & Co.

Fabrics

Acme
New Haven Moving
Rennert

Farm

Creutzburg
Sears Roebuck

Flooring and mats

Aborn Rubber
Allied Mat & Matting
Allstate Rubber
American Hotel Register
Banner Mat & Products
A. N. Brabrook
C&H Distributors
Import Specialists
Koffler Sales
Pawling Rubber
U.S. Mat & Rubber
Wilcox International

Furniture

Adapto Steel Products
Adirondack Direct
Alfax Mfg.
Ascot Steel Equipment
Business & Institutional Furniture

Carts

Able Steel Equipment
Adapto Steel Products
Adirondack Direct
Advance Products
Alfax Mfg.
American Hotel Register
Arista Surgical Supply
Ascot Steel Equipment
Business & Institutional Furniture
C&H Distributors
Crown Discount
Daroma Restaurant Equipment
  (Metro)
Empire Food Service Equipment
Equipto
Fidelity Products
Fred Hill & Co.
A. Liss & Co.
HG Maybeck
Prima Education Products
Professional Kitchen
Scan Plast Industries
Scientific Products
Shure Mfg.
Steele Canvas Basket
Arthur H. Thomas
Wilcox International

C&H Distributors
Crown Discount
Frank Eastern
Elkay Products
Equipto
Fidelity Products
Hallowell
Fred Hill & Co.
A. Liss & Co.
Lyon Metal Products
Manhattan Ad Hoc Housewares
Penco Products
Republic Steel Industries
Shure Mfg.
Standard Equipment

Glass (plate and wire)

C-E Glass
Central Dental Supply
Pittsburgh Corning

Janitorial equipment

Accessory Specialties
American Hotel Register
Beam Supply
C&H Distributors
Crown Discount
HG Maybeck
Charles Parker
Steele Canvas Basket
Tubular Specialties Mfg.
Wilcox International

Kitchen equipment

Ajusto Equipment
American Hotel Register
Brookstone
Conran's
Cooks Supply
Daroma Restaurant Equipment
Edward Don & Co

Empire Food Service Equipment
H. Friedman & Sons
L&B Products
Manhattan Ad Hoc Housewares
Metropolitan Wire Goods'
Professional Kitchen
Scan Plast Industries
Shure Mfg.
Vandermolen
Wilcox International

Lighting RLMs

Abolite
American Hotel Register
Appleton Electric
Arista Surgical Supply
Benjamin Div. - Thomas Industries
C&H Distributors
Central Dental Supply
Charrette
Conran's
Crown Discount
A. Liss & Co.
Manairco
J. C. Penney
Sears Roebuck
Smith-Victor Corp.
Thunder & Light
Times Square Theatrical
Wilcox International

Marine and automotive

Defender Industries
Max Finkelstein
Goldberg Marine
Huffy Automotive Products
Manhattan Marine & Electric
MG Mitten
Motion Performance Parts
J. C. Penney

Office furniture and equipment

Able Steel Equipment
Adirondack Direct
Advance Products
Alfax Mfg.
American Hotel Register
Business & Institutional Furniture
C&H Distributors
Cayne Equipment
Charrette
Crown Discount
Frank Eastern
Wilcox International

Outdoor furniture

Advance Mfg.
Algoma Net
American Hotel Register
L. L. Bean
Conran's
Tucker Duck & Rubber
Wilcox International

Restaurant equipment

American Hotel Register
Cooks Supply
Daroma Restaurant Equipment
Edward Don & Co.
Empire Food Service Equipment
H. Friedman & Sons
L&B Products
Metropolitan Wire Goods
Professional Kitchen

School supplies and equipment

American Athletic Equipment
American Hotel Register
C&H Distributors
Childcraft Education
Crown Discount
Edmund Scientific
J. L. Hammett
Jayfro
Learning Products
Prima Education Products
Standard School Equipment

Scientific and lab glass and supplies

Ajusto Equipment
Arista Surgical Supply
Central Dental Supply
Darby Dental Supply
Edmund Scientific

Interstate Dental
Keystone Optical
Lab Glass
Scientific Products
Silverman's Dental Supplies
Arthur H. Thomas

Seating

ABC Foam Rubber Center
Adirondack Direct
Advance Mfg.
Ajusto Equipment
Alfax Mfg.
Algoma Net
American Hotel Register
L. L. Bean
Belson Mfg.
Business & Institutional Furniture
C&H Distributors
Charrette
Conran's
Crown Discount
Equipto
Standard School Equipment
Sun Glo
Tucker Duck & Rubber
Vandermolen
Wilcox International

Steel shelving

Able Steel Equipment
Adapto Steel Products
Ascot Steel Equipment
C&H Distributors
Cayne Equipment
Elkay Products
Empire Food Service Equipment
Equipto
Fidelity Products
Hallowell
Fred Hill & Co.
A. Liss & Co.
Standard Equipment

Storage:
clothing

Alfax Mfg.
American Hotel Register
C&H Distributors
Crown Discount
HG Maybeck
Result Mfg.
Scan Plast Industries

Storage:
containers, glass, etc.

American Hotel Register
Arista Surgical Supply
Brookstone
C&H Distributors
Charrette
Childcraft Education
Conran's
Creutzburg
Crown Discount
Darby Dental
Early Winters
Keystone Optical
Lab Glass
Manhattan Ad Hoc Housewares
Outwater Plastics
Result Mfg.
Scan Plast Industries
Scientific Products
Silverman's Dental
Storage Concepts
Arthur H. Thomas
Wilcox International

Storage:
wall systems

John Byron Displays
C&H Distributors
Sid Diamond Display (Grab)

Empire Food Service Equipment
  (Metro)
Metropolitan Wire Goods
Professional Kitchen (Metro)
Scan Plast Industries
Storage Concepts (Schaeffer)

Tables and work surfaces

Able Steel Equipment
Adapto Steel Products
Adirondack Direct
Advance Mfg.
Alfax Mfg.
American Hotel Register
Arista Surgical Supply
Business & Institutional Furniture
C&H Distributors
Cayne Equipment
Crown Discount
Elkay Products
Equipto
Fidelity Products
Hallowell
Fred Hill & Co.
Industrial Products
L&B Products
A. Liss & Co.
Lyon Metal Products
Penco Products
Scientific Products
Shure Mfg.
Standard Equipment
Arthur H. Thomas